Eighteen East 74th Street

An Autobiographical Novel

Lawrence H. Staples, Ph.D.

CHIRON PUBLICATIONS · ASHEVILLE, NORTH CAROLINA

www.ChironPublications.com

Interior and cover design by Danijela Mijailovic
Printed primarily in the United States of America.

ISBN 978-1-63051-887-5 paperback
ISBN 978-1-63051-888-2 hardcover
ISBN 978-1-63051-889-9 electronic
ISBN 978-1-63051-890-5 limited edition paperback

Library of Congress Cataloging-in-Publication Data

Names: Staples, Lawrence H., author.
Title: Eighteen East 74th street : an autobiographical novel / Lawrence H. Staples, Ph.D.
Description: Asheville, North Carolina : Chiron Publications, 2020. | Includes bibliographical references. | Summary: "I'm an 88-year-old retired Jungian Analyst. I wrote this book to share a lifelong struggle to free myself from the powerfully dominating influence of my mother, something Jung more elegantly described as "The Battle for Deliverance from the Mother." It's a battle I now doubt can be won, although an uneasy truce may be achievable"— Provided by publisher.
Identifiers: LCCN 2020049004 (print) | LCCN 2020049005 (ebook) | ISBN 9781630518875 (paperback) | ISBN 9781630518882 (hardcover) | ISBN 9781630518899 (ebook)
Subjects: LCSH: Staples, Lawrence H. | Psychoanalysts—Biography. | Jungian psychology. | Mothers—Psychology.
Classification: LCC BF109.S73 A3 2020 (print) | LCC BF109.S73 (ebook) | DDC 150.19/54092 [B]—dc23
LC record available at https://lccn.loc.gov/2020049004
LC ebook record available at https://lccn.loc.gov/2020049005

Gate C22

At gate C22 in the Portland airport
a man in a broad-band leather hat kissed
a woman arriving from Orange County.
They kissed and kissed and kissed. Long after
the other passengers clicked the handles of
their carry-ons
and wheeled briskly toward short-term
   parking,
the couple stood there, arms wrapped around
   each other
like he'd just staggered off the boat at Ellis
Island,
like she'd been released at last from ICU,
   snapped
out of a coma, survived bone cancer, made it
   down
from Annapurna in only the clothes she was
   wearing.
Neither of them was young. His beard was
gray.
She carried a few extra pounds you could
   imagine

her saying she had to lose. But they kissed
  lavish
kisses like the ocean in the early morning,
the way it gathers and swells, sucking
each rock under, swallowing it
again and again. We were all watching—
passengers waiting for the delayed flight
to San Jose, the stewardesses, the pilots,
the aproned woman icing Cinnabons, the man
  selling
sunglasses. We couldn't look away. We could
taste the kisses crushed in our mouths.
But the best part was his face. When he drew
  back
and looked at her, his smile soft with wonder,
  almost
as though he were a mother still open from
  giving birth,
as your mother must have looked at you, no
  matter
what happened after—if she beat you or left
  you or
you're lonely now—you once lay there, the
  vernix
not yet wiped off, and someone gazed at you
as if you were the first sunrise seen from the
  Earth.
The whole wing of the airport hushed,
all of us trying to slip into that woman's
  middle-aged body,

her plaid Bermuda shorts, sleeveless blouse,
   glasses,
little gold hoop earrings, tilting our heads up.

ACKNOWLEDGEMENTS

First, I wish to express gratitude for my dreams. They have enriched my life in many ways. They have been a great source of comfort, insight, and guidance. They have also inspired me and stimulated the creative thought and imagination that resulted in this and other books and pieces. I also feel grateful for dreams that sometimes seem to have connected me to others, to life and the universe in ways I could never have achieved on my own. Without my dreams, I would have experienced a poverty far deeper and more painful than the material poverty I experienced as a child, which I still fear. More importantly, perhaps, as I age I find that my dream life is considerably more interesting, exciting, and uninhibitedly fun than my real life.

Without Karen Farley, who worked her beautiful, incredible magic in editing the piece, this book would have languished like a diamond in the rough, longing to be polished and seen. And thanks to my wife Nancy, who supported my writing in many ways and was especially helpful as always with amazing insights and suggestions.

I used to say to patients that it didn't seem fair for them to have to pay me because I learned so much from them. But it's the truth. Their experiences and insights with their own mothers were especially important in helping me see and understand some of the very subtle and nuanced ways that my mother exerted such a powerful influence on my life, one difficult to see in real time but nonetheless so deep and powerful that it survived my growing estrangement from her, an estrangement that began in my teens and deepened throughout my life, even after her death.

PREFACE

Because all autobiographies contain fiction, some more and some less, I call this piece an "auto-biographical novel." Written at my advanced age, it is also likely my last book and may serve as my obituary when the time comes. In this role, it may be somewhat more open and embarrassingly honest than most obituaries, which wisely are not very honest at all.

This book is the result of a cascade of fantasies and memories that flowed from the intense work I did on a very powerful late-life dream. The writing itself produced insights that helped me deal with the lifelong psychological struggles depicted in the book.

Thus, this book is mostly about me. Accordingly, I wrote it in the first person, using the "I" as I imagine myself to be. While I am clearly the scribe, it feels as though some background entity that I refer to as my "self" is the author and is speaking through me. It also feels as though some uninvited voices have shown up, have inserted themselves into my process and are competing to speak. I am carefully watching, listening, and attempting to sort the inner hubbub. Some voices win out, and I wonder what causes the winning voices to win. When I was younger, I was barely, if at all, aware of these competing internal voices. At eighty-eight, I'm not only aware of them, but I find sorting them to be quite challenging and befuddling.

The narcissism of the piece, its materialistic flavor, its boastful vanity as well as its self-effacement, are all reflections of and flow out of an early psychological wound which all my life filled me with anxiety, insecurity, guilt, and self-absorption. This piece is an attempt, very late in life, to continue the healing of that wound by creating a pool in which, like Narcissus, I can see myself in reflection. It is an attempt to make a better mirror in which to see myself than the mirrors I had growing up. It is an effort to become conscious of more of myself than I previously knew and, hopefully, continue the increase in consciousness and healing that didn't begin in earnest until the second half of my life.

In the course of my efforts to heal, I have been attracted to a view of narcissism expressed by Norman Mailer, who saw and wrote about narcissism in a way that is quite different from the standard psycho-analytic view, which casts it as a psychological disorder. In contrast to the psychoanalytic view, Mailer believed it was an oversimplification to think of narcissism as self-love. In his view, narcissism has fundamentally to do with a relationship to one's self. It is an inner dialogue between an observer and other parts of himself, where one self is absorbed in studying the other parts. Mailer felt that, seen this way, narcissism actually enhances the creative process. I think it can also heal. We'll see. My attraction to Mailer's view is also likely a defense whose purpose is self-protection; even an orange needs a peel to protect its potentially nurturing but vulnerable inner parts. The peel, of course, can also conceal what's rotten inside. Often we're fooled in both directions by outer appearances. I think we just never know for sure.

I feel quite uneasy about releasing for publication this often disparaging and muddled picture I've painted of myself with its surreal mix of fact and fantasy. But, then, I said to myself, "What the heck? At eighty-eight, what can they do to me?"

This piece began with the following dream and the thoughts and fantasies that flowed in its wake.

THE DREAM

It was a big dream, despite its brevity and simplicity. The words "Eighteen East 74th Street" appeared without any embellishment or commentary. The dream came while I was in New York City recovering from knee replacement surgery. In the dream I knew the address was somewhere in Manhattan. The dream was so powerful that I couldn't help thinking about it and wondering what it might mean, if anything.

Very soon after the dream I Googled the address. It was an upper east side townhouse that was for sale for $28.5 million. I could hardly believe that the house I dreamed of was actually for sale. This coincidence seemed pregnant with meaning. And it set off a cascade of magical thinking and rich fantasies. Surely, I thought, God wants me to have this amazing house. And if God wants me to have it, he will provide the money. I'm eighty-eight years old, and while my wife, Nancy, and I are comfortable financially thanks to royalties from mineral rights in Oklahoma, there's no way that we could afford either a mansion like that or a lifestyle that mirrored its magnificence. So, my mind seized upon a lottery jackpot as the only way we could afford the glittering new life the dream led me to imagine. Surely, I thought, God would give us the lucky numbers.

The more I thought about the dream, the more my fantasy life exploded, like some inner nuclear chain reaction. All I had to do was close my eyes and the movie began, a movie of life in seven stories, eight bedrooms, five baths, elegantly furnished, filled with expensive art and statuary, with a view from its roof of New York's Central Park, all stunningly impressive. The fantasies kept me from getting to sleep, and, when I finally did get to sleep, woke me up at all hours of the night. They would not leave me alone. During the day I was exhausted from lack of sleep, but even in waking hours the fantasies would flood me and keep me from tasks that needed to be looked after and, from a practical standpoint, seemed much more important than my imaginings. It was as if I'd hooked a big fish, and it was hauling me out to sea against my will. I couldn't stop it. It was too big, and I was too small.

I couldn't help wondering why this dream and all these fantasies would come to me so late in life. Did the dream and the fantasies have a purpose and meaning? Or were they just psychic vapors that floated in and out of my mind and meant nothing? Or, if they meant something, were they pointing to something that was supposed to manifest in the reality of my outer life? Were they pointing to something connected to my inner life, past life, or both? Was it a call to somehow make my inner hut into a splendid mansion? If the dream was about my outer life, the chasm between my actual outer life and the dreamed-of life was so huge it could only be bridged by some fateful event that made me rich enough and energetic enough to do all that would be necessary to build the life of my dreams. If it was about my inner life, the canyon between the actual and the dreamt also seemed huge.

Thus far, my fantasies suggest the dream was about outer life. Daily, I imagine the wondrous details of actually living in that house with the grand lifestyle it suggests. I also imagine the complicated details of obtaining the necessary money and securing and managing it.

The fantasies are in two steps that intermingle. First, I fantasize about winning the lottery. I think about how large the jackpot must be to support the dreamed-of life. I begin to imagine that after taxes, we'll need $30 million to buy the house and its very expensive and tasteful furnishings, along with a vacation house at The Landings in Fort Myers in order to escape the harsh New York winters. We'll want to add a swimming pool. And I figure we'll need at least $700 thousand per year or more just to cover taxes, insurance, and maintenance. We'll also need a full-time maid and cook since we'll want to throw elegant dinner parties and invite all our friends to enjoy the splendor. We'll even invite our friends Enrico and Linda to come from Florence. And, of course, when friends are in New York, we'll want to entertain them with Broadway shows and other extravagant diversions that only New York City can provide. I also imagine the satisfaction we'll get from seeing the looks on our friends' faces when they walk through the door of our impressive house the first time. After all, it's that gleam in another's eyes, that look full of approval, wonder, and amazement at one's achievements, that makes one try to accomplish great things. Isn't it?

What I call "that look" is, perhaps, the thing I most yearn for in life. It may even be the thing most, if not all, people seek. It's a profound wish, embedded in an infant's unconscious, to repeat that gleam—and particularly the ecstatic feeling that went with it—that we saw for the first time in our mother's eyes as she looked at us adoringly, like the Magi, with an unconditional love that suggests she's looking at something divine. "That look" touches us so profoundly because her eyes reflect back to us an image of our self that is as truly who we totally are as we will ever see, unless we are lucky enough later in life to find a better mirror. "That look" revealed no reservations about us. "That look" reflected back to us an unconditional, pristine, unphotoshopped image of our selves. We got "that look" before we had achieved anything. Mother loved us because she found us lovable just as we are. We got "that look" despite our dirty diapers. We got "that look" despite our expression of qualities that later mother would despise, disapprove of, or frown upon at best. A frown from her had the opposite effect of "that look." (In fact, the potential to incur the frown, the contrasting opposite of "that look," is actually an important part of what gives so much meaning and power to "that look.") Later, we ourselves would come to despise, disapprove of, and reject those frowned-upon qualities when they raised their ugly heads in us, qualities like selfishness (waking our exhausted momma so she could feed us), noisiness, irresponsibility, laziness, lack of ambition, unproductiveness, demandingness, uncleanliness, disorderliness, unreliableness, anger, impulsiveness, honesty of feeling, incontinence, helplessness, dependence, and the sexual enjoyment of fondling and sucking nipples and breasts.

That frown, the very first second at which it appeared, was a critical moment psychologically. It was the precise turning point at which we split into two, opening the door to the psychic basement into which the frowned-upon stuff is shoved and stored. And most of it stays there, until later in life when we might, if we are lucky, begin to retrieve these rejected parts of ourselves. The frown is the moment the shadow forms and we lose our wholeness. To our chagrin and consternation, however, these shadow parts occasionally become troublemakers and slip back through cracks in the door in ways that embarrass and humiliate us, or worse, until more frowns, from without or within, cause us to herd the shadow parts back into the cellar as best we can. In some cases, our shadow qualities may elicit a frowning response from others, but often we have so internalized the response that we play it back ourselves, in self-condemnation.

But before any frowns ever flashed across mother's face, there was "that look," a brief moment of pure love. Receiving it is one of the great moments of life. But great moments are great precisely because they are moments. They are a fleeting experience, especially the unconditional part. Socialization began early, with more or less severity, and soon we only got that adoring look, that gleam in her eye, when we did something that pleased her immensely. The high that we get from that gleam, the warm rush that suffuses our bodies and minds, addicts us in the same way the first drink addicts an alcoholic. And, like an alcoholic, if need be, we'll sacrifice ourselves on almost any altar to repeat that feeling. We'll study long hours to the point of exhaustion if good grades please her. We'll keep our room clean no matter how tired we are. We'll work ourselves to death, if necessary, to get that promotion we know would please her and cause others to give us "that look," if only for a brief second. We become hopelessly addicted to achievement of those things she approved of and pursue them relentlessly, even long after she is dead. If we ever needed proof of the power of the small, "that look," like an atom, is it.

"That look," which was given so freely at the beginning of life, becomes harder and harder to get. It gets weaker and less frequent than that first look. We learn we have to get it the hard way; we have to earn it. Even in its weaker form, however, it still yields quite a high. It may be like coming down from heroin to alcohol, but there's still a warm buzz. Unfortunately, sometimes, we lose "that look," even in its weaker forms, almost entirely as mother gives it to younger siblings as they come along. We get displaced. But "that look" is a drug we need, and, as it becomes harder to get, we look for more sources. Over time, we make others our surrogate mothers: teachers, bosses, spouses, friends.

In my case, I was displaced by a younger brother. While I wasn't conscious enough in real time to understand or give a name to what was happening, I learned later in my Zürich analysis that my anger at and resentment of my brother were the early symptoms. My unconscious brought me a dream that helped me finally understand my dethroning and the anger and hurt it unleashed. The dream inspired me to write the following poem:

Déjà Vu

I'd give my life to get the look
She gave him yesterday.
I'd give my life to get the look
That finally made me pray.

That look of adoration
That no one can describe,
That look of love and reverence
I wish I could imbibe.

A look that is so special,
It brings me close to tears,
A look engraved within me
To last a thousand years.

It's deeper than an ocean
And richer than a mine,
A look so sadly exquisite
Only worship can define.

A look that causes envy
And weakens every knee,

When it is for another
And not at all for me.

And painfully I see this look's
A mirror of her heart,
That cannot lie, or fake the fact
She loved him from the start.

She loves him, no denying,
No matter what the price.
She can't conceal the feelings
That lie behind those eyes.

Some people look for money;
Some people for success.
Some people look for fancy things;
And some for happiness.

But all I ever looked for
Was the look she gave to him,
And when I saw he got it,
I thought my life would end.

'Cause I have looked a thousand places
And everywhere I roamed,
I saw ten thousand faces
And turned ten thousand stones.

Then, I saw her give that look
I'd sought for many years.
And suddenly remembered,
With sadly falling tears,

Where first she gave that lovely look,
That deeply wounded me,

Some forty long, long years ago
And never set me free.

Now I knew that nothing's changed,
A case of déjà vu,
The look I craved, she gave another,
As mama did to baby brother.

Mama's Reply:
Why should I owe you the look
I gave your baby brother?
Who are you to claim or hook
The feelings of another?

Feelings aren't for sale or lease;
They're owned by their possessor.
Feelings are a special piece
And God the only lessor.

Unless you think
You're God above
And make a claim
For all the love.

Let me give away my looks
To anyone I wish,
And you can do the same some day
When love finds you a dish.

This does away with jealousy;
Gives love its proper place,
And sets us all completely free
In harmony and Grace.

That's fair enough for everyone;
Sets everything in place.
Puts God at center, like the sun,
In universal space.

While the dream and the poem it inspired helped me understand the power of "that look" and the hurt and anger at its loss, it really didn't, as I had hoped it would, ameliorate my feelings of resentment toward my brother. I could understand intellectually that the way I felt was neither his fault nor mine. But I couldn't change the way I felt. It showed me how the need for "that look" is so profound that its loss feels like a threat to survival, even if it really isn't. It's so palpable that the "enemy" cannot be forgiven no matter how much one may wish to do so or how much that "enemy" deserves forgiveness.

Another crushing memory may help explain why forgiveness is so hard. My mother often called me Ronnie, my brother's name. I remember clearly a conversation in which she called me Ronnie and I corrected her. I would say, "You just called me Ronnie. I am Lawrence." She replied, "Now, Ronnie, I didn't call you Ronnie." It was hopeless and, perhaps, her way of passive aggressively venting anger at me and exacting revenge for a betrayal of her, which I will discuss later. Of course, it is utterly irrational to blame my brother for her slights, but at eighty-eight years of age, after years of work on myself, I think it is safe to assume that the feeling is just what it is and that it will remain so until it isn't.

Mother's reply in the poem contained a liberating idea that helped me realize why I became so addicted to "that look." She said her look didn't belong to me. It belonged to her and she gave it where she pleased. The point goes to the heart of addiction, why it happens and what we have to do to get free of it. We become addicted when we deeply need something that we don't own, when we have to get it from someone or something outside ourselves. In the larger world, we can see the phenomenon in America's addiction to Saudi oil. We remain addicted until we can supply that need from within. The shale that lies deep beneath the surface in Oklahoma and elsewhere in America became the key to liberating us from Saudi oil. Once we discovered this source of oil on the inside of America, we no longer were dependent on oil from someone outside of America. We were free of the addiction to the Saudis. Similarly, if we want to be freed from the obsessive pursuit of "that look" from others, we have to somehow find a way to give "that look" to ourselves. We need to find the magic mirror within that permits us to get "that look" from ourselves. Mother's eyes were our first mirror. We saw ourselves through them. She looked at what she saw and reflected it back to us. But the mirror was likely accurate for only the briefest of times. It could see us with all our beauty and flaws and reflect us back without judgment. It saw us as we were. Soon, however, the mirror became distorted by judgment. It came to reflect how mother wanted us to be rather than how we were. And we then distorted ourselves in an attempt to once again experience "that look" from a mirror that now reflected only one side of ourselves, the approved side.

I also suspect there is a sexual content to "that look." The feeling that goes with it is close to ecstasy, even orgasmic. I think that a brief feeling that we associate with the experience of love briefly passes between the giver and the recipient of "that look."

I believe "that look" can have a dark side as well. I have wondered if a profound deficiency of "that look," and the feeling attending it, is what causes some people to yearn so deeply for it that they will kill for it or hurt others for it. I've had patients who reported their experiences of sadomasochism, or S&M. In the S&M ritual, there is usually a "top" and a "bottom," a dominant and submissive one. I've been told that the high feeling comes when pain reaches a peak and there is a moment of reversal in which the "top" becomes "bottom." At that moment of peak pain, there is an ecstasy that produces something like "that look" and the feeling that goes with it in both participants. I know it sounds irreverent and incredible to say this, but it seems as though there is a kind of conversion experience in which dominance becomes submission when submission becomes dominance. We know that conversion experiences produce a palpable high and that that high can resemble sexual feelings. I've heard stories of serial killers in which they go through a similar S&M process. It's "that look" in their victim's eyes and the erotic experience it produces that leads them to kill again and again. Just at the moment of death there is visible in the victim's eyes the *petite morte*, or little death, the French phrase for orgasm, a moment in which the ego disappears and the self comes through. The killer briefly sees himself. It's a testimony to humans' incredibly profound need for "that look" that those who have too little of it will kill or hurt others in order to satisfy that need. I can admit to murderous thoughts about my brother and father, who represents the qualities in me that might keep me from getting "that look." Thank God, those murderous thoughts never incarnated.

The incomparably exquisite feeling that one got from "that look" is also likely what addicts are seeking in alcohol or gambling or drugs. Similarly, they also have to find an inner source that replaces a feeling they have only been able to find outside, in a bottle or a card game. They also need a magic mirror to produce that feeling from within.

We need a magic mirror because we are actually afraid to see ourselves as we truly are. We need a mirror in order to see ourselves as we are without that sight shattering us. I suspect that to see ourselves as we truly are without something mediating it is to see God, the totality that contains all the light and the dark that is expressed in all God's creation. Although our unconscious may contain the totality that is God, we can't become God because we can never see or know it all. That's an important part of what keeps us human and limited. We can make progress, but we can't get to the end. We are all aware of the biblical admonition that to see God is to die. We can neither look at God nor ourselves totally without dying. It's especially our dark side that is terrifying. It is terrifying because we learned from mother that the effect of displaying our dark and unacceptable side would be the loss of her love. If mother doesn't love us, we can't survive—or so we feel. To lose mother's love is to lose God's love, as mother is our first image of God. While the fear or the fact of having no money is quite painful, it pales by comparison to having no love.

To see our dark side, we have to look at it indirectly with something mediating its force. As the myth of Perseus tells us, we can only do that with a mirror. It is difficult for us to look directly at the real source of our fear without shattering. It's one thing to look at my fear of flying; it's another to look at the fear of my own evil, to look my own Medusa[1] in the face. Even someone as powerful as Perseus[2] couldn't do that. He had to see Medusa, his dark and evil side, as a mirrored reflection in his shield. That's why therapists mirror, so that people can see their "faults," their dark side, the parts of themselves unacceptable to authority, from a safer perspective, in reflection as Perseus did, rather than head on. I'll talk later about how we can find and use our own magic mirror to get "that look" and the feeling that goes with it.

To return, as I must, to the exhaustingly dreamed-of life at Eighteen East 74th Street that I had been

---

[1] Medusa is a mythical figure who personifies evil. She is one of three Gorgons, who according to myth had wings and snaky hair, most horrible to mortals. No man can behold her and live, for whoever looked at her turned instantly to stone.

[2] In the myth of Perseus, the shield given him by the goddess Pallas Athene served as a mirror that permitted him a sufficiently clear view of Medusa that he was able to lop off Medusa's head without actually having to look directly into her face. According to the myth, Medusa's face, when looked at directly, had the deadly power to turn the viewer to stone.

conditioned to believe would get me "that look," I am now imagining that, among other things, we also need a limo service to get us about town. And, we can't forget a NetJets subscription to take us to our house in Fort Myers, to Oklahoma to look after our oil interests, to the Super Bowl, Wimbledon, the French Open, the Final Four, the NBA finals, and the Masters. In my imagining, I don't forget the need to fly to Durham, North Carolina, once or twice a year to see Duke play basketball in Cameron Indoor Stadium, especially the Carolina game. I imagine making a big contribution to Duke so that we can get tickets. Our attraction to Duke basketball and coach K is a long story, but the essence is that Nancy and I fell in love while watching Duke win the national championship in 1991. And not to neglect some other interests, I imagine visiting the Bayreuth Wagner Festival, the Montreux Jazz Festival, the Cannes Film Festival, and the Pyramids and other wonders of the world. I would take pictures and present slide shows of all these phenomenal venues for our friends. While they'd be watching the slides, I'd be watching their faces for you know what. Of course, my annual Christmas letter would be filled with news of all these visits, acquisitions, and accomplishments.

In Oklahoma, we'll want to buy back the pecan orchard my family had to sell during the Great Depression. The orchard, on Caddo Creek, is still beautiful, and I imagine we'd enjoy taking friends out to see it. I imagine mentioning how we had tenant farmers take care of the orchard for us. This effort to hold on to "the good old days" would have a

Chekhovian feel about it that our literary friends would probably appreciate with "that look," perhaps less moving than momma's first look, but still quite animating.

We'll also need fancy new cars to leave in Oklahoma and Fort Myers to get about when we are visiting those places. BMWs or Mercedes will probably do, with the ones for Florida being convertibles. I don't think we'll want cars in New York. The limo service should suffice and be much easier and safer.

I also imagine wanting to spend a few weeks in Paris every year, taking a few friends along with us. I imagine them being impressed with my French, not to mention our private jet. Impressing them with our jet and our Paris digs and seeing the looks on their faces would likely be an important reason for flying our friends with us to Paris, just as it was a motivation for inviting them to our stunning house in New York.

I've thought about buying an apartment in Paris so that we could leave stuff there and not have to pack when we visit. For the time being, I've dismissed that idea, as I worry we may get so much property to look after that we won't have time for more interesting things. We'll just rent a fabulous apartment through HomeAway/VRBO.

I continued to imagine what I would do with all that money. For one thing, I imagined giving generously to things we value. Out of deep gratitude for what they did for me early in my life, I'd like to contribute a significant amount to Thomas Jefferson School, the prep school in St. Louis that gave me a full scholarship to attend, to Harvard, which also awarded me a full scholarship, and the Jung Institute Zürich, from which I also graduated, becoming a Jungian psychoanalyst. I hate to admit this, but I suspect that one of the reasons for giving to Harvard now is also to grease the path to a membership in the Harvard Club of New York City. That's a pretty impressive place to take people in order to bring "that look" to their faces. I could probably get in without the contribution, as Bruce, my roommate from Harvard, is still alive and belongs to the New York City Harvard Club. Still, I see the contribution speeding things along. I would also want to contribute to a fund which offers scholarships to worthy students in Ardmore, Oklahoma, where I grew up and where we have lived for the past few years. I imagine giving at least a million to each of these educational institutions. I also wouldn't mind seeing the look on the faces of some Ardmoreites when they hear or read about my educational gifts, although, unfortunately, most of those whom I've harbored a lifelong wish to impress are now dead.

Some of these thoughts sound like thinking rather than fantasies. But thoughts about the future are fantasies. They're not real yet. The same is true about thoughts about money I don't have yet. And thoughts about the past are also fantasy, since, except for my memories, the thing that was real then is now dead. Most of the numbers cited in this piece are imaginary except my age and the cost of some houses. And sometimes it's just images that come. I see in my mind's eye all the details of this fabulous house, flying in a private jet, friends in our fabulous dining room, and, of course, "that look" on their faces.

In my florid imagining, I've added all this up in order to determine the size of the jackpot we would need to win. I say "we" because my wife and I always buy lottery tickets and have agreed to share any winnings. After taking all these financial needs into account, I think we would feel safe if the jackpot yielded us $100 million after taxes. That requires a jackpot of about $300 million before taxes, since we would take the cash payout rather than the annuity. After buying the houses and furniture in New York and Fort Myers, we'd need a million or two to put Christa, my oldest daughter, in a super-nice nursing home and provide for her care for life. And we'd want a few million for Amanda, my youngest daughter, so that she'd have enough to buy the house and car of her dreams and have some income from the remainder.

All of these items together would take close to $45 million, leaving us $55 million to invest and cover our living expenses. Nancy could live another twenty years or more. If we got no return on investment, we could, over a twenty-year period, spend $2.75 million per year after taxes before we exhausted the original $55 million. If we could invest the $55 million safely at 3 percent, we would earn about $1.65 million per year, and even more if the interest were compounded. If we felt like taking a bit more risk, we could increase the income by investing some of our money in quality stocks. Or, if we needed to, we could take $2.75 million per year from principal.

We would definitely have a lot of operating expenses. As mentioned, we'd need at least $700 thousand per year for maintenance, insurance, and taxes. (We'd likely keep our house in Oklahoma for our periodic visits.) As mentioned earlier, we'd also need a maid, a chef, and probably, as I am now imagining, an administrative assistant to free us of much time-consuming detail. I'm imagining needing at least $200 thousand per year for these items. We'd also want to give Amanda, my daughter, $500 thousand per year so that she and her family can have an abundant, worry-free life. Then there would be a NetJets subscription. I imagined needing an $800 thousand subscription to take us to all the events and places we'd like to go. That would leave about $700 thousand per year for other living expenses and charitable contributions. Actually, we could do much of this even if we won less money. We could leverage our house with loans and obtain several years of operating expenses that way. But our preference is for a jackpot big enough to permit us to have this experience without having to worry, maneuver, and cut corners.

Interestingly, at the end of twenty years living all that fantasy, if one of us were to be alive, we'd still have a Manhattan townhouse and Florida and Oklahoma houses that would likely have appreciated considerably. By that time someone likely would have inherited the houses. I imagine they'd probably have to sell the Manhattan house in order to have enough to live.

The above line of imagining gives at least a sweeping view of how we'd spend the money. But much more imagining would be required to get the money, secure it, and invest and manage it.

To begin with, I think about how anxious I'd feel about protecting the winning ticket, until we could cash it in at the lottery office. First my wife and I would need to sign it so that no one else could use it, if they found it or stole it. But what if a draft blew it out a window? I saw a movie once in which the winning lottery ticket blew out a third-story apartment and was never found. Keep windows closed. What if we were burglarized? Get ADT to install foolproof home security to supplement the pretty good system we already have. We would want cameras at each door and motion-activated spotlights on all sides of the house. Do we put the winning ticket in a safety deposit box until we can get to the lottery office? Or do we put it in a fireproof box we have at home? Or do we keep it on ourselves at all times? Or do we just go immediately to Oklahoma City and stay locked up in a nice hotel room until we can get to the lottery office? We'd have to stay safely ensconced in the room until the very moment we would leave to cash in our ticket. To do this, we'd have to get all our food from room service. I also imagine carrying the winning ticket in my billfold, which I'll keep under my pillow at night. I might even take my .38 police special along for extra comfort. Many people in Oklahoma carry. Do we make copies of the ticket? Actually, that wouldn't do any good. You have to present the original ticket no matter what. Then, I would worry about the lottery people cheating us. So, I imagine getting a lawyer as a witness to go with us to pick up our check and make sure all the paperwork is correct. We would also want our lawyer to do whatever is necessary to keep us anonymous. We definitely don't want anyone to know we won, although buying the houses in New York and Fort Myers would raise eyebrows. We'd have to come up with an answer for that. I'm thinking I'd rather say we had a windfall in our oil and gas income. That somehow doesn't sound as big as a lottery jackpot. In saying that, I feel really conflicted. I want friends to be impressed with our things and approve of our lifestyle. And I want them to admire me and give me "that look" when they first see our grandiose life. I just don't want them to know exactly how much we have. I also don't want to appear to be so rich that people would be asking for money. That's probably wishful thinking. Once I give a large amount to schools, they'll incessantly be dunning me for more. Oh, the burdens of wealth. But I imagine I could handle it and bear it, especially with an administrative assistant to take care of the grunt work.

Once we get the big check in our hands, I've had to imagine what to do next. After much thought on this subject, I've imagined that a private bank, like Bank of America's U.S. Trust, could best manage this much money. One problem is that the nearest U.S. Trust office to Oklahoma City, where we get our check from the lottery office, is in Tulsa or Dallas. I worry about that long drive with that big check or having to stay in a hotel overnight with that much money. If we could get our check before noon from the lottery office, we could probably make it to Dallas or Tulsa before closing time. We prefer Dallas. It's closer to where we live. Worrying about losing the check might be needless. The lottery people would likely replace the check if lost or stolen, but I need to put that on a list of things to ask them about in order to be absolutely sure. It's possible we could deposit the check in a regular Bank of America office in Oklahoma City by using CDARS, Certificate of Deposit Account Registry Services, but I would need to confirm they could handle this large amount.

Even the U.S. Trust in Dallas would not be the one we would want to work with on a daily basis. In Dallas (or Oklahoma City, if CDARS works), we'd simply deposit the money and have them set us up with an account manager in New York City, where we'd be living our imagined opulent life. After imagining our drive to Oklahoma City and back to Dallas, I found myself thinking we should get a new, very safe, and reliable car to make the trip. It would probably be quickest and easiest if we were to pick up a Toyota Land Cruiser at the local Toyota agency. The Land Cruiser is big, comfortable, and safe. It would be a shame to have car trouble while driving to claim our winnings or while transporting the huge check to the bank. I imagined a Toyota, because there are no Lexus, Acura, or, surprisingly, Cadillac dealers in our small town. New as our wealth would be, I imagined a Cadillac as a bit *nouveau riche* for the old money feel I would wish to more tastefully project in order to get "that look" from our friends.

I imagined the U.S. Trust account manager helping us with a lot of things that might otherwise be quite difficult to manage. Investment decisions have to be made and implemented. I'm imagining now that, at our age, seventy percent of our investments would go into treasuries and top-rated corporate bonds, while thirty percent would go into blue chip common stocks of the highest quality. Because we would likely become New York residents, subject to oppressive tax rates, we would also want investments to provide us the most tax efficient income as well as potential for capital gains. We also would need easily accessible cash in rather large amounts to take care of monthly operating expenses. Our account manager could probably also help us set up an efficient bill paying system.

The account manager, in my imagination, could also help us buy Eighteen East 74th Street by recommending a knowledgeable realtor and real estate lawyer with reputations for honesty and integrity. The bank knows such things, information that is not easy for ordinary people like us to come by. He could probably also help us with locating an administrative assistant, chef, and maid, as well as home maintenance people and a reliable limo company. We'd need assistance in locating a good estate attorney in order to get our wills and trusts updated to reflect our New York residence. And I imagine our banker could even help us find tickets to plays, concerts, and sporting events. I assume they will be well remunerated for these services from fees they would charge for managing our investments and banking needs. Actually, my old Harvard roommate could be quite helpful in a number of these matters.

All of the above imaginings, thoughts, and fantasies are only the briefest summary, the tip of the iceberg so to speak, of all that reeled through my head on this subject. Therefore, even if all the fantasies recorded above were to become manifest in my life, the sum of all those that were not manifested would actually be much, much larger. The inside is always bigger than the outside. An architect that builds a great building certainly scrapped more ideas, concepts, and design details than actually went into the building. He also probably imagined many ideas and designs for other structures that never saw the light of day. What most painters or musicians or writers imagine far exceeds what they actually produce. The value of an artist's work tends to be based upon what he actually produces. But this may be a false valuation. Perhaps his artistic worth, even his self-worth, is the total of the inside and the outside, the part that was manifest plus the part that was modified or rejected or set aside or held in abeyance. I like that idea because it makes me feel bigger and more worthwhile. What I've actually produced and achieved in my life seems paltry by comparison.

The psychiatrist C.G. Jung spoke often of the conflict between spiritual and material values both in our inner and outer lives. A central tenet of Jung's thinking was that the first half of life should focus on success in the outer world, but that the second half of life should be spent becoming successful in our inner life. For him, the inner life is the large part of ourselves that was unlived in the first half of life. It is the part of us that we didn't know about or that was not allowed, because emphasizing it would have interfered with our achieving outer success. I think that many Jungians, including me, believe that the inner work is the most important, and that a successful life ultimately depends upon a successful development of the inner life. My ongoing dissatisfaction with my outer life at age eighty-eight has caused me to question the supremacy of the importance of the inner life. It has made me think that inner and outer, spiritual and material, should be equal players on life's stage.

Jung could speak from a platform that is quite different from most, if not all, of us. Early in the first half of his life, he married Emma Rauschenbach, reportedly the second richest person in Switzerland. From the time he married her, he was relieved of the challenge of earning a living in order to pay the bills and acquire the finer things of life. Without his earning a penny, he could enjoy an impressively beautiful home, have maids and nannies, butlers and cooks, yard men, fine cars, chauffeurs and a yacht built for ocean travel. He also could afford secretaries and other assistants to help him with his work and writing. When he became ill at midlife and began the long dive into the unconscious that resulted in the development of Jungian psychology, he could do that work without concern for money. He had all the advantages of wealth without having to work for it.

It is likely, of course, that no one else, rich or poor, could have produced what he did in his life. His mind, work ethic, and creativity led him into unexplored realms and left the world with a great treasure of thought and insight. While I doubt anyone else could have achieved or contributed what he did to psychology, doing all that inner work in the second half of life was probably not as daunting as it is for those without his kind of material safety net. If most of us had a prolonged illness at midlife, as he did, we'd soon be broke. And while most could never accomplish what he did, even if wealthy, many could probably accomplish more if their time and effort were not distracted by the need to do paying work in order to live even a modest outer, physical life.

Jung had a spectacular inner and outer life. Yet, his prescriptions for a successful life tend to favor the development of the inner life. That may explain, at least partially, why most people attracted to Jungian psychology are introverted. But it's easier to believe and say that the development of the inner life is paramount if you have a grand outer life safely in place and feel virtually invulnerable to assault. It reminds me that, when I was in training, a fellow student stated to a teacher how important he felt getting a diploma was. The teacher, who was a diplomate and well credentialed, scoffed and told him what he learned was most important and that you don't really need a diploma. In truth, they are both important. Scoffing about the need for something one already has is easy. It's like rich people scoffing at the importance of money.

In Jung's case, I am suspicious that the enormous wealth which permitted him to live a spectacular outer material life also caused him to devalue the importance of the outer life. He could spend much of his adult life paying increasing attention to his inner life without concern for his physical existence.

At midlife, influenced by Jung as I was, I had come to believe that my inner life was the secret to fulfillment, that the skin of outer success and the strong need for it could gradually be shed without a great sense of loss. However, the dissatisfaction I still feel with my outer life, despite all my inner work, leads me now to think that the outer may be just as important to our ultimate fulfillment. Extroversion may be as important as introversion. Many Jungians would resist that assertion. My dreams suggest that no matter how much I achieve on the inside, I still need the grand house, the money, the prizes, the recognition, the spectacular outer life to complete the earning of "that look." While I have paid attention to my outer life, I probably did not devote enough to it to be as successful as an important part of me wants to be.

Part of me looks down on this conclusion about the outer life and has increasingly belittled it since I first began to read Jung in my late forties. If I am truthful about my feelings, however, it seems to make no difference to those feelings whether or not part of me looks down on the outer stuff. It's still very important to another part of me. The relationship of outer to inner may be different for each individual person depending upon his biography. But this is the way it seems to be for me.

Of course, all my conclusions are subject to change. I feel now that only fate can deliver me the outer life I still hope for. That has probably always been true; I just wasn't aware of what I now believe to be fate's huge power in our lives. It will be interesting to see what happens, but I doubt there is a lot of time left to watch the dreams and the movie unfold. And they will unfold as they will, whether I like the movie or not.

The spiritual/material tension that exists both in our inner and outer worlds is poignantly portrayed in a television series called *Un Village Français* (Azémar & Krivine, 2010), a documentary about the Nazi occupation of France during World War II. In one episode, the Nazis have rounded up scores of Jews and are holding them in a schoolhouse that is totally inadequate, creating horrible living conditions. In addition, the Jews had been arrested suddenly with no advance warning, so only a few had had the time and foresight to take a little food with them.

Soon the hunger was so great, especially among the children, that the adults tried to find a solution. A middle-aged woman came up with the idea of taking an inventory of the small amounts of food that some had and distributing this somehow to the children. Some thought this was a communist idea. Finally, they said that the woman who had the idea of inventorying and redistributing food should go to the rabbi and ask him to resolve the dispute. The woman resisted at first, saying the rabbi was occupied with praying and meditating, but eventually she approached the rabbi. The conversation had to be translated as the rabbi was Polish and spoke no French:

Rabbi: What does she want?

Woman: Sir, I'm trying to help people here. The Polish people here say they won't share food with others here unless you say it is okay. They say sharing is like giving to beggars.

Rabbi: You are helping beggars.

Woman: Not at all.

Rabbi: You are spreading discord.

Woman: All I want is solidarity to stand together.

Rabbi: Are you a believer?

Woman: No. Does that matter? We simply need to find a way to get food for children.

Rabbi: It matters a great deal, Madame.

Woman: You say you want to fight injustice.

Rabbi: But actions are pointless if you don't understand the reason. You must always give meaning to actions.

Woman: The children don't need meaning; they need food. They need to eat.

Rabbi: If we give them food, they will be happy. So will we, but without understanding the truth. Evil is being done to us. But the real evil is within us. And only prayer and meditation can help us win, triumph, overcome.

Woman: Can you help me or not?

Rabbi: On one condition. Only if we have a prayer and meditation service with all participating. (Azémar & Krivine, 2010)

Obviously, materiality is even harder to renounce in favor of spiritual values when the material object in question is food for starving people. In my case, the materiality that tempts me is far above the subsistence level, but I still struggle with the question of whether my dream should be interpreted as a kind of prophesy of something valuable that will happen in the external world or be viewed as something valuable and meaningful that is happening within. In comparing the inner and outer possibilities, though, I must acknowledge that the odds of winning the jackpot are nearly one in 300 million. For comparison, the odds of being hit by lightning are one in 13,500. Logic tells me that the odds of winning a Mega Millions or Powerball jackpot are so small that I'd better look for the meaning and value, as well as the fun, on the inside, where neither moths nor rust can corrupt. The value, as an inner thing, would lie in a place safe from thieves or from expropriation by authorities. It would be secure even if America went broke. Hence, the odds on the inside are probably better than the odds on the outside.

Still, it's a little disappointing to have to think of the value as inner. Even if in reality it turned out not to be so, it seems that actually winning a jackpot and being seen living the lifestyle that went with it would be much more fun and exciting than only dreaming and fantasizing about it. On the other hand, I suppose one could hypothesize that whatever value is inside, small as that might be, it is worth more than a jackpot that was not won and houses that were not bought or lived in.

To think of the value of the dream appearing on the inside, I have to think about the meaning of dreams and their interpretation. Jungians generally believe that dreams, among other things, are compensatory in nature. You dream of what is missing in your life, not what is present. So, an inner dream of riches would be to compensate for some kind of poverty.

In my case, I'm not rich, but I am far from poor. However, earlier in life I experienced much poverty and deprivation. I was born in Oklahoma in 1932, in the depths of the Great Depression. So, my early experiences make me imagine that the dream compensates for my *fear* of being poor, rather than my actually being poor. While it may be somewhat neurotic for me to fear being poor in my present circumstances, the life experiences that caused the fear entered me early and were very real. In those early days the fear of not having enough was neither neurotic nor paranoid. And it's very possible that the fear of being poor may have been the psychological factor that has kept poverty at bay, at least so far. At eighty-eight, the poverty I was conditioned to fear is going to have to run pretty fast to catch me before I go on to a place that can truly only be imagined.

Growing up, we literally had no cash money except my dad's $30 monthly government pension check, which he received because he'd lost his arm during the first world war. And that money was always at risk, because my dad was an alcoholic. On the first of each month, my mother and grandmother, my father's mother, with whom we lived, were on constant alert to be sure they got to the mail and my dad's check before he did. Still, since he had to endorse the check before they could cash it, he always grabbed a chunk to spend at the taverns, where he drank daily, usually while playing checkers and dominoes. A few times he actually beat them to the mail and got away with the entire check. Then, I would go with my mother to all the beer joints he frequented, and she would send me inside to try to find him and preserve at least some of the cash before it became urine. My mother always waited outside. It was a humiliating experience accompanied by much anxiety, as it was the only money we had to pay bills for food we couldn't grow ourselves and for essentials like electricity and gas. My mother and grandmother were constantly wringing their hands in anxiety about having enough to meet our basic needs. Daily, this fear was in the air. It permeated our lives. Even when they were able to get my father's entire check, things were very tight.

Although we lived in town, we had an extra lot, which we used to raise chickens for meat and eggs and to grow a garden to supply vegetables to eat and can for winter. Thank God my grandmother owned the house outright so there was no rent or mortgage to pay. We could afford to have chicken once a week on Sundays. The other days we ate vegetables only. I can remember my mother telling me to go to the grocery store across the street and ask for the lettuce trimmings to feed our chickens. That was also embarrassing, and the chickens never saw the lettuce leaves. About the only time we had salad was when we were able to get the trimmings. To give you an idea of how undernourished I was, when I was in high school I was six feet, three inches tall and weighed 130 pounds.

In grade school, I spent a lot of time at my friend Buddy's house. It was an awesome house compared with mine. And the food, the fresh fruit, the steaks, the desserts and candy, all of which they had in abundance, they generously shared with me. I suspect they took this abundance for granted. I could only dream of having it in my home.

My dad had a wily way to get more money to support his drinking. He would buy cartons of cigarettes on credit at various stores until one after another they cut him off for not paying his bills. Whenever he succeeded in buying on credit, he would then take the carton of cigarettes to a beer joint and sell them to the owner at half price in exchange for beer. One really embarrassing experience was when he asked me to go into Gravitt's Drug and get a carton of cigarettes on credit for him. Mr. Gravitt refused, saying I needed to get my dad to pay his bill before he could give us more cigarettes. I was probably eight years old when that happened, but the humiliation of being turned down and dunned for my dad's bill and for his obvious dishonesty was seared into my memory. It is one of those memories that contributes to my *fear* of being poor or even of paying bills late. I'm still so neurotic about that that I almost always pay bills early.

When I was about twelve, my father got a job as janitor at the Oklahoma State Employment Office. He made me help him in the evenings after they closed. One evening I was sweeping the floor when I heard a knock at the front window. Peering in were Rutherford Brett, a classmate, and his parents, passing by on their way to a movie. Janitorial work is honest work, but at that age I was ashamed not only of doing it, but of friends seeing me doing it with my father. In general, I was ashamed of my father. He dressed in khakis, often urine-stained or soiled from his drinking sprees. He did not hold jobs very long as he was unreliable and would miss work because he was drunk or too hung over. He got fired from the employment office soon after my friend and his parents saw me helping him.

I was also ashamed of our house. It looked okay from the outside, but the inside was a scene of disrepair. Wallpaper was torn. Paint and varnish peeled from the woodwork and floors. Carpets and furniture were worn. We never had company except for other family members. We didn't want others to see my father or the inside of our house. I suspect all families with alcoholic members are pretty secretive and closed off. I remember sitting on the front porch once when a car pulled up and discharged my father. He was dead drunk and was crawling on his hands and knees as he tried to get up the terrace to our house. Neighbors were also on their porches observing the pitiful scene. I literally pulled him up the terrace and carried him into the house. I was probably fourteen or fifteen years old by then.

All this led to consuming feelings of shame about our house, about the janitorial and other menial work my father did, and about my father and his appearance and failures. The shame reflected an enormous false pride harbored not only by my mother and grand-mother, but by my entire extended family. I can remember my aunt Wilma getting married and a week later running her new husband off and divorcing him because he was in their driveway in his tee shirt washing their car on Sunday. She could not stand the idea of neighbors seeing his "disgraceful" behavior.

In order to have some spending money for myself and to help the family, I began to work when I was six years old. My grandmother would parch pecans and make fudge and divinity candy. She'd put small amounts in cellophane packets, put them in a little wicker basket with a handle, and send me off to sell them in downtown offices. I actually did pretty well selling candy, and some months I brought in about as much as my father's pension. I was pretty proud of that, and I got a lot of praise from my mother and grandmother. Later I had other jobs like a paper route, working at J.C. Penney, and working at a bank.

I held these jobs for many reasons, to pay the bills and help feed the family, to have a little money of my own, and, not least of all, to earn praise and "that look" from my mother. In fact, the more I think about the dream of Eighteen East 74th Street, the more I am coming to question my initial interpretation that it compensates for my fear of being poor and un-successful. I'm now leaning toward believing the dream was more about a fear of losing the love and admiration of my mother than of actually being poor. Having no love may be scarier than having no money. The dream may serve as a symbol of how rich and successful I feel I must be in order to maintain her love and esteem. While growing up I heard my mother (and grandmother to some degree) decry my father on a daily basis. She condemned his drinking, irrespon-sibility, inability to hold a job and make a living, inability to provide, unreliability, shabby appearance, laziness, dishonesty, and general profligacy. She was disgusted with him, disapproved of him, and looked down on him. She thought he was the reason why we were poor, and she blamed him for our poverty. I could hear the scorn in her voice and see it in her face. Unless I was badly mistaken, it didn't sound like she loved my father, and I wanted to be nothing like him if I could help it. The message for me was that if you want to be loved, you have to manifest all the trappings of success by being very well off and prominent in the community. Viewed this way, my obsession with having a lot of money, an impressive house, and a lavish lifestyle would have been the means to an end, rather than the end itself. The end so desperately sought was to be loved, to get "that look."

I remember hearing both mother and grandmother talking about the men they admired, men who were the opposite of my father in almost every way. They only looked up to men who were very wealthy, though often they expressed their preferences in rather unsophisticated ways. The admiration might be voiced in statements like: he wears suits and ties to work, he works in an office, he has a desk, he drives to work, he's a good provider, he is very smart and works with his head, his wife and family have a big house or fancy clothes, and so on. Often I would hear my mother say to my sister, "You need to make sure you find a man who is a good provider." My sister actually did that. She married an engineer who did very well. Then he came home at night and beat the hell out of her.

My mother and grandmother had attitudes about manual labor that might have parallels in the European aristocracy's feelings about peasants and their work. They rarely had anything good to say about blue collar people who worked with their hands, despite the reality that many of them were adequate providers and might be more loving fathers and husbands than some of the richer men they admired. But my young mind probably didn't make these class distinctions then.

We seem to be wired to be drawn to things that get us approval and love, especially things that bring that glint to our parents' eyes. That's why later in life we try to achieve things that will bring that same gleam to the eyes of friends, colleagues, and neighbors. In my family, mechanics, plumbers, and farmers were not on the list of approved occupations. Doctors, lawyers, bankers, ministers, and executives, particularly those connected with oil, were admired. My father was pretty good at mechanical things when he was sober. Despite having only one arm, he could fix a whole array of things including toilets, washing machines, and lawnmowers and their small motors. I could have learned a lot of useful things from him that would have helped me later in life. But I was conditioned by my mother's and grandmother's attitudes to shun tasks involving manual labor. It left me with a permanent disability, dependent upon others to do those things for me. Later in life I paid through the nose for help with things I could easily have learned to do for myself when I was young. Fortunately, I could afford it. My attitude for a long time was: pay someone to do the grunt work you don't like or are unable to do.

There was a deep irony in the incredible false pride harbored by my mother and grandmother. Much of what they valued and admired was missing from their lives. My mother's husband, my grandmother's son, was a drunk, couldn't hold a job, was slovenly looking, and, when he did work, it was with his hands (or hand in his case). Our house was a mess. We didn't own a car until I was fifteen. We barely had enough to eat or wear. It was hard to hide these facts in a small town like ours. Before the Depression, while my grandfather was alive, my grandmother had been well off. But she had sold most of his land and run through most of his money by the time I was born. Even so, she maintained the affectations and pretenses of her previous life, one that no longer existed. For example, she still had the dresses she had worn to church, dresses that were truly fine ten years earlier. She could wear the satin and lace of her more prosperous years, but now it had an aged, worn look that fooled no one. In our small town the truth got around despite her futile efforts to conceal the abject reality of our existence, the huge gap between who we once were and who we had become.

To be fair to my grandmother, she was very smart and had some genuine artistic gifts. She could play the mandolin, and she won blue ribbons every year at the county fair for her hooked rugs, crochet, and embroidery. She also had a head for business, but, by the time I was born, she could find no way to use it in a deeply depressed economy. Before she married my grandfather, she had founded and owned a millinery store in Denton, Texas. That was in the 1880s, quite a notable feat for a woman in those days. She had met my grandfather there, and they married and moved to Ardmore, Indian Territory, where he built the biggest and best grocery business in town. He was known as "Porter Staples, the Redheaded Groceryman." His brother, my great uncle, had arrived in this part of Oklahoma before my grandfather. He'd actually been the founder of the town of Ardmore. My grandfather and my grandmother were a good team, and their business was very successful. They acquired a lot of property and farmland. At one time they owned not only our house, but the two houses on either side of us.

My grandfather was what they called a "periodic alcoholic." He had a predictable cycle. He would stay sober for thirteen months, then check into a hotel and stay drunk for a month. While he was drunk, my grandmother was able to hold things together until he sobered up again. But these cycles took their toll, and he died drunk when he was fifty-five. Slowly, as the Depression worsened, the money slipped away, and the property was sold off piece by piece until all that was left was our house and a 120-acre pecan orchard. During the Depression, the tenant farmer had no cash, and he paid us with half the pecans harvested each year. When he brought pecans, the whole family would sit around a table and crack nuts with little hand machines made for that purpose. For weeks we would crack and peel pecans, which we sold to stores. Those were the pecans my grandmother parched for me to sell in offices. Eventually even the farm had to be sold. Fortunately, my family retained partial mineral rights, and I am the lucky owner of those today.

I absorbed the high value my mother and grand-mother placed on wealth and success at a very early age. An obsession with prosperity suffused my being, took up a permanent place in my subconscious, and had a lifelong effect upon the direction of my life and the choices I made. This background influence on my life was mostly unconscious until later in life, when I underwent a long psychoanalysis, but, looking back, its effects were apparent even at an early age. Almost eighty years ago, I recall, I did something that reflected this subconscious belief that I had to become wealthy and successful if I were to be loved, admired, and accepted.

I was eight or nine years old when Jacqueline Chesser moved to Ardmore from North Dakota. She was so pretty and was my first love. She lived in a rented apartment about a block from my house. I thought she was the prettiest, smartest girl I had ever seen, and we really liked each other. Unfortunately, her father moved them back to North Dakota after about a year in Ardmore. It was a very sad time for me. I missed her so much and yearned for her helplessly. Several months after she had gone, I wrote her a letter begging her to come back. I told her that I had become very wealthy and would send my chauffeur for her. I wrote that I would build her a mansion on Sunset Drive, in the best part of town, that I would buy her a Cadillac and spoil her with clothes, furs, and other luxuries. It was a wildly absurd, hyperbolical letter that reflected my belief I could only be loved, could only get "that look," if I could be wealthy enough to provide a woman a splendid life. Anything less would leave me alone and unloved. No wonder I still dream of owning a beautiful mansion in New York City!

The letter to Jacqueline was also a clear example of a complex that essentially dictated the choices I made and the direction of my life. Freud used the words "Oedipus Complex" to describe an unconscious competitive drive, beginning early in a little boy's life, to beat father out for mother's love. One way they imagine winning is to have sufficient money to enable them to give their mommies all the nice things in life that their fathers can't provide. It is a deeply rooted complex that drives many men to become good providers as adults.

While writing about my Oedipus complex, my earliest memory in life slipped into my mind. I'm imagining that's because there is a likely relationship between that memory and the Oedipus complex. My earliest memory is of being alone under a neighbor's car with my toy duck. The fact that the toy that I remember so vividly is a duck seems symbolic. Ducklings are known for their tendency to imprint on the first object they encounter in life, usually the mother. They follow that object wherever it goes. Pictures of small ducks following their mother are often used to illustrate the process of imprinting. I suspect this early memory reflects my vulnerability to my mother's conditioning and my lifelong tendency to follow, outside of conscious awareness, her central wishes and values. I was never aware of this tendency at the moment it insinuated itself into my decisions. It was only in retrospect that a clarifying insight would, usually as a result of my therapy, writing, or journaling, often make me conscious of its influence.

My need for "that look" and the love it implied increased my vulnerability to my mother's influence and caused me to watch her face intently and listen carefully in order to catch the nuances in her demeanor and voice that indicated things she admired and approved of. One thing became clear early. The first time I brought home a report card with mostly A's, her eyes and face lit up. My mother called her sisters and brothers to tell them the good news. For a time, I became a kind of trophy son she paraded before her relatives like a prize bull. She reveled in my success and promise. She knew that doing well enough in school to get into college was likely the only way up and out of our abject lives. I think she also saw me as a kind of golden boy who gave her and my grandmother hope for redemption of the family that, due to to my father's behavior, had fallen from community respect and approval. Of course, their reactions did not escape my ne'er-do-well father's notice. In my Oedipal struggle with him, I'm fairly sure my mother's seeing me as her golden boy diminished me in his eyes.

My father seemed to hate me. When I was five, he and a drinking buddy took me out fishing with them at Lake Murray. They were both pretty soused, and at some point, my father grabbed me and threw me in the lake. It was one of the most terrifying moments of my life. No one had ever tried to show me how to swim, and my father made no attempt to save me. I was on my own, and some will to survive led me to thrash and splash around until my father's friend pulled me out. I never forgave my father. Terrifying, though less so than my near drowning, were the frequent savage beatings my father administered with a conveniently available razor strap, kept at the ready, suspended from a nail in the bathroom.

To put my adherence to my mother's central values in perspective, I actually resisted her and trespassed her values in many small ways. There was all that stuff that boys do and mothers often disapprove of: masturbation, sex, vandalism, petty theft, smoking, drinking, cursing, and more. I was pretty good at hiding my offenses but was occasionally caught and shamed. My deep guilt didn't keep me from transgressing again. It just made me miserable for having done so. Despite my dad's alcoholism, the family history of the disease, and my mother's and grandmother's constant admonitions against it, I began to drink with friends when I was twelve years old. But I didn't think I was weak like my father, and I felt I would never succumb to alcohol as he did. Besides, I think that at some level, I felt that abstemiousness was only important to them because they believed it would interfere with success. I was aware that my mother and grandmother admired many men who drank moderately but were wealthy and successful.

Despite my deviations from some of mother's values, her most important ones clearly influenced me. She wanted me to have a good, high-paying job, become wealthy, have an impressive house, dress well, be respected in the community, and project the appearance of success. Although she wouldn't call it that, false pride was almost always at work in her and contagiously so in me. So, while I wandered off her approved path in many small ways, she had created a maternal undertow that pulled me toward her valued goals all my life. Often, I was unaware of this undertow until some retrospective insight permitted me to see it. Even though I became increasingly alienated from my mother beginning in my early teens, her powerful undertow has continued to exert itself throughout my life. Because of this fateful connection to my mother, I have spent much of my life in what Jung referred to as "the battle for deliverance from the mother" (Jung, 1989, p. 9). Let me be clear, however, about where the real battle must and does take place. It's with the mother complex that remains in my head, persisting long after my estrangement from and the death of my outer mother. The fight is with the mother that took up residence in my psyche long ago. While my complex is based on my real mother, it is not exactly her. The complex represents my real mother plus amplifications, interpretations, and perceptions supplied by something else in my psyche. For example, I would guess that the dream of Eighteen East 74th Street is a very exaggerated view of my mother's goals for me and of the goals she would have actually felt or articulated. My dream of a spectacular life, like the letter I wrote to Jacqueline Chesser when I was eight or nine years old, is likely my mother's wishes and goals on steroids. My actual mother would probably be quite proud of the life I have had and even of the more modest one I have now. I'm the one who believes he needs Eighteen East 74th Street and the life of grandeur that goes with it in order to be loved. She planted the bean; something other than she, something within me, grew the bean stalk. The witch that offered me the poisoned apple is in me. It's important to bear in mind that when I write "mother" I'm referring mostly to the one inside. Although she is an inner construct, I've spent much of my masculine energy in her service. And serving her, at least serving her as I interpreted it, separated me from myself and kept me from myself or, perhaps, more accurately, parts of myself.

From time to time my children would tell me they did something because they knew I expected it. I was often puzzled, as I would be unaware of having placed those expectations on them. But I cannot rule out the possibility that some grimace or smile or slight gesture on my part led them to decipher an expectation emanating from me that I was totally unconscious of. No doubt this was also similar to how my mother's expectations and values insinuated themselves into me. It seems to me that the voices of my parents, predominantly my mother, are always in me, more or less, trying to assert themselves and influence my thoughts, feelings, and behavior.

Other powerful figures who somehow touched me deeply, like my grandmother, the headmaster of my prep school, my boss in business, my analyst, and others, are also in there and are often speaking through me without my knowing it. I remember once at a party a colleague from my company said to me: "You sound exactly like Phil Brownell," my dear old brilliant boss who was president of the company.

By the way, my boss, Phil, was an amazing person from an amazing family. Working several years for him was one of the richest experiences of my life. He was one of seven children born to a professor at the University of Nebraska. His mother was a minister. All seven children were Phi Beta Kappa in college. Phil went to Yale Law School and finished at the top of his class. He was editor of the law review and was awarded membership in the Order of the Coif. His brother Herbert was Attorney General under Eisenhower. Phil is the only person I am consciously aware of wanting to imitate (unsuccessfully, I must say). He had a razor-sharp mind and could write beautifully. Despite his power and wealth, he was not pretentious. He bought his suits at J.C. Penney, drove Fords, and lived rather modestly. He was respectful of others and kept his integrity pretty much intact despite the huge pressures and temptations that touched his office. While no one is completely honest, he seemed to be exceptionally so compared with others I knew well. I really loved Phil, but, of course, I was unable to imitate him given the strong undertow I later realized my mother exerted on me. Others could at times hear these inner influences. I'm some combination of all those voices and the particular mix of those voices is likely what makes me unique. I suspect that is true of most of us.

When I make decisions, it feels to me that one of these voices, be it my mother, my grandmother, my old boss, my analyst, or others, is always temporarily dominant. It wins. If that were not so, it would be difficult to make decisions. When I am indecisive, it is because there is too much equality among the competing voices. Until one rises above the clamor, I tend to be paralyzed and to live in a state of great tension. In my case, it is often mother who wins, but others also succeed at times. Again, I suspect most people experience something similar to that.

By the time I was a sophomore in high school, my mother's ambitions for me had grown into full blossom, and my effort in school intensified. I strove increasingly to maintain good grades. Good grades always briefly brought me "that look" or some semblance of it. It was the only way I knew I had pleased her. In our family, there was never any hugging, touching, or other overt expression of love. No one ever said to me, "I love you." Even birthdays were never celebrated. It was very hard to know where you stood. The deep need to become wealthy and successful in order to win and keep my mother's love, expressed by "that look," created in me a deep resolve that drove my thought and effort. I agreed that education was the most promising way for me to achieve the things she approved of.

As a result of the increased effort to excel in school and accomplish other things that might make me attractive to a college, I began to make straight A's, was elected to the honor society, and was ranked first in my class. In addition, I lettered in track and wrestling and was named president of my class. This effort paid off, and I was selected to go to Boy's State. There, I was nominated for and ran for president. I was defeated, but my consolation speech, and the fact I got the highest grade in the civic exams that all attendees had to take, impressed the Boy's State faculty and led them to pick me and one other student to attend Boy's Nation in Washington, D.C.

It seemed that one thing led to another. As mentioned earlier, Thomas Jefferson School, a private college preparatory school in St. Louis, was offering a full scholarship to high school students in Oklahoma. They asked a professor at Oklahoma University to recommend someone. The professor had been a key faculty member of Boy's State. He had been impressed with me and recommended me for the scholarship. A teacher from Thomas Jefferson came to Ardmore to interview me, and, after obtaining very high scores on a battery of IQ and other tests he administered, I was offered the scholarship. It covered everything except the cost of transportation to and from the school. I could cover that with summer work before school started. It was an exciting time. My teachers, friends, and family were very proud and complimented me, and I loved basking in that momentary limelight.

In my first interview with the headmaster, he told me that if I were to do well at Thomas Jefferson School, I could almost certainly get a scholarship to Harvard. That came as a shock. The idea of attending Harvard had never entered my mind, even with my soaring ambitions. I did do well at Thomas Jefferson School and on the college boards. As the headmaster had predicted, I received the Lawrence H. Coolidge Memorial Scholarship to Harvard. It was a four-year scholarship that covered everything but spending money, clothes, and transportation, assuming I always maintained sufficiently high grades to graduate *cum laude*, which I did. To cover spending money, I worked twenty hours per week in one of the graduate school cafeterias. Thanks to an aunt who gave me money for some extras at college, I was able to get and accept an invitation to The Hasty Pudding Club, a membership rarely achievable for a scholarship student. Her financial assistance also helped me become a member of Sigma Alpha Epsilon, the only national fraternity at Harvard. SAE carried some social weight but was not as prestigious as Hasty Pudding or finals clubs, but I lacked the necessary pedigree to be accepted into finals clubs.

The truth is that, despite all this unexpected advancement, I saw having a scholarship as evidence that I was poor. My pride was so great and so false that I never mentioned to other students that I was on scholarship. I couldn't help but feel that, like my mother, other students at Harvard would not approve of me if they thought I was poor. They, of course, would not actually have felt that way, but, because of my inner wiring, I couldn't help thinking or feeling that they would.

During the latter part of my senior year, the headmaster of Thomas Jefferson School invited me to accompany him and two other students on a three-month tour of Europe. I told my aunt about the opportunity and she offered to pay for the trip. The students going on the trip were from well-known and wealthy families. One of the guys was a Burden, a New York family related to the Vanderbilts. Except for me, it was a pretty elite group. It was an amazing educational experience as we visited London, Paris, Madrid, Rome, and Athens. The headmaster was a classics scholar and taught us much about the history of places we visited, especially Athens and Rome. It was a great piece of luck for me. I could never have had this experience without my aunt's help.

During my senior year at Harvard, I applied to and was accepted by Harvard Business School. The aunt who had helped me to a lesser degree in college actually paid for my Harvard Business School education and gave me a car to use while I was there. In many ways, she made my life easier and better. In a sense, from Thomas Jefferson School onward, I was a very poor boy who got a very rich boy's education.

My relationship with Aunt Pearl began when my brother was born and grew in closeness and strength over the years until I felt she was more of a mother to me than my actual mother. In a way, Aunt Pearl and I were made for each other. She had no children, having lost her only child when he was two years old. She was unable to have children after that. She needed a son. I needed maternal emotional support and financial help if I were to accomplish some of my important goals. Over time, she became "mom," and I became "son." Her influence on my choices in life was much less than my actual mother's influence, but her emotional and financial support made us outwardly closer. However, our relationship became a source of humiliation for my mother, and she felt betrayed by Aunt Pearl and by me. My appreciation for Aunt Pearl was genuine, but at the same time I knew that my embracing her heightened my mother's sense of betrayal. To some extent, I'm sure I turned toward my aunt as a way of expressing the deep anger I felt from losing my mother's love and "that look" to my younger brother.

When I received my MBA, Harvard asked if I would be interested in staying on and becoming a research fellow. I was too impatient to start making money and rejected that idea. Upon graduation, I was offered a job by a Fortune 500 company, and before I was forty became what was at that time the youngest corporate vice president and officer in the history of the company. In the first few years of my business career, I drank heavily and was in the early stages of alcoholism. By the grace of God, when I was thirty-seven, I had what I came to believe was a kind of a spiritual experience that freed me of the need for alcohol for good. I came to believe, rightly or wrongly, that one result of the experience was that God, the name I give to that psychic entity, infused my ego with new strength sufficient to withstand the need for drugs or alcohol to relieve pain and make me feel better. The spiritual experience and my stopping drinking liberated a huge amount of energy, which in turn led to much achievement at work and rapid promotions.

In my late forties, however, I became very ill, and I nearly died before having open heart surgery. It was a wake-up call. The illness was clearly a result of my not taking care of myself. I always worked incredibly long hours, didn't maintain a healthy diet, didn't make time for exercise, and took few vacations. I was always stressed and felt under tremendous pressure to produce good results in the part of the company that I managed.

After surgery, I lost interest in work and felt unhappy, depressed, and afraid. These feelings and the near-death experience began to open my mind to making changes in my life. The idea of change, necessary as it seemed, was nevertheless difficult to embrace. By this time in my life, I had almost everything I had been taught would make me feel happy, loved, and admired. I'd married, and my wife and I had two daughters. I was not a good father. I was too obsessed with my work and making money. I wasn't able, or didn't take the time or make the effort, to teach them things they needed to know to get on in the world. Fortunately, my wife was there for them and took care of them. We were very well off financially. We had pretty much all the material things we could reasonably want. It created for me a great dilemma. I was afraid to give all this up and equally afraid not to, if I were to have anything near a normal life expectancy. Eventually, I decided to find a therapist with the hope that a good one could help me let go of the old way and find a new one. After three years of therapy, I was able to discover a new direction that was sufficiently appealing to overcome the anxiety of letting go of a life that provided so much that was important to me.

Another powerful dream played a role in preparing me to walk away from past achievements and create a life that would be slower-paced and healthier. The dream led me to write a story that involved replacing the Arch of Triumph[3] in Paris with a huge

---

[3] Paris's Arch of Triumph sits at the top of the Champs Elysees in one of Paris's most prominent plazas. From the time the Arch of Triumph was constructed until recent years, the plaza was called the *Etoile*, the French

gold bidet. To replace the Arch of Triumph with a lowly bidet was a good symbol to guide my surrendering an ambitious pursuit of achievement and glory in favor of a more modest path that was more protective of my health and well-being. It's probably a pretty good symbol for many people at midlife who have slaved and achieved much but have run out of gas and interest. The term "midlife crisis" applies well to the condition.

Replacing the inner Arch of Triumph as a personal symbol and the guiding star for our life with a new symbol, the lowly bidet, can feel redemptive. It is a significant personal transition, beckoning us now to live some parts of our life that were unlived because of our implacable pursuit of outer achievement. For me and many men, this meant giving time and attention to the development of the feeling side of ourselves and our relationships. We could begin to till the fallow field of feeling that had been ignored while we unrelentingly plowed another field that was narrow and one-sided. The truth is that we often have to specialize, prioritize, and focus on a single, narrow field if we are to be successful in the first half of life. But in that process, we leave untilled large parts of ourselves that yearn to be seen and developed. If we succeed mainly with our thinking function, we are often quite unaware of feelings, especially those that would get in the way of practical things. With a new symbol to guide us, we

word for star, a guiding symbol that directs our lives and leads us to something sacred, as it did for the wise men. It is now called Place Charles De Gaulle.

may now be able to work an uncultivated field that has grown in richness but is almost completely undeveloped. The fallow field lies only *in potentia* until we plow it and make its contents manifest.

As part of my therapy, I read a lot of psychology and became very interested in the subject, being especially attracted to Jungian psychology and its ideas about midlife and its problems. When I turned fifty, I resigned from my company and applied to the Jung Institute in Zürich to enter training to become a Jungian psychoanalyst. There were a number of reasons for making the change besides my health. I was attracted to my new career by my interest in the subject as well as my wish to help people and to contribute to the community. In addition, I wanted to help myself. I wanted to earn enough money to have a comfortable physical life and pay my bills. Of course, the vaingloriously absurd wish to become a famous psychologist like Jung passed briefly through my mind. I probably thought that achievement would gain me "that look." Obviously, nothing even close to that happened.

There was another reason for wanting to become an analyst that, perhaps, trumped the others. I knew that analytical training required, as a component, a long and deep analysis. I felt there was some craziness in me so brutal that it would drive me, at a self-sacrificing pace that nearly killed me, in order to achieve its goals. I had learned something about this craziness in my prior therapy but felt a need to learn more if I were to have a less stressful life and a normal life expectancy.

One thing I learned in my analysis was that an important part of the reason for being able to let go of my old life, besides a wish to stay alive, was that the new life would make me a doctor. Doctors were at the top of mother's approved lists. My mother herself had become a licensed practical nurse. She virtually worshipped doctors. In fact she named me after the doctor who delivered me, and he later encouraged me to become a medical doctor. But I was unable to make myself like the medical profession. She admired doctors not only because they made a very good living, but also because they usually lived in impressive houses and had high status in the community. They were special. A Ph.D. might not quite meet her standard, but at some level it must have felt close enough to help me accept the idea of being a psychoanalyst. In some ways, mother was still running my show. I say "show" because appearances were important to her and to me. The depth of the need to be a doctor, however, can be seen in the type of Ph.D. I managed to obtain. In Switzerland the Ph.D. is awarded only by federally authorized universities. The Jung Institute, a private educational institution in Switzerland, is not authorized to award the Ph.D. degree, despite the fact that the training is long, rigorous, and of very high quality. Demanding theses must be written and defended. Americans who train there can get a Ph.D. equivalency by submitting their course work and theses for analysis and comparison with the academic work required for a Ph.D. in American universities. Americans hiring foreigners for research and other work often don't, without such an analysis and comparison, know what the foreign academic credentials mean. While there were some very practical reasons for getting a Ph.D. this way, such as meeting licensing and insurance requirements, the appearance of the degree was also very important to me. I came to feel that practicing as a psychoanalyst and having a Ph.D. would provide a level of income and respect that would satisfy that inner maternal standard. Despite the sometimes practical, sometimes neurotic, and sometimes pretentious reasons for becoming an analyst, I do think I learned a lot in my training and was able to help a lot of patients. It always was a source of pleasure when I thought I had really helped someone. But sometimes, I felt I hadn't helped no matter how much I might have tried. That was painful. I do believe I gave the work my best effort except on occasional days when for some reason or another I might have been very tired or distracted.

Because of my lack of previous training and experience in psychology, it took me nine years to complete my training at the Jung Institute. I stuck it out in order to get the best training and to support all the reasons I noted above for entering training in the first place.

My income now was entirely from investments and was a fraction of what it had been when I was an executive. While I was in Zürich, my younger daughter went to college and my wife went to the Culinary Institute of America to pursue interests she had held in abeyance while raising a family. Our lives and interests diverged, and we never got back together again. Eventually, we divorced.

Over time, the cost of my education and that of my daughter and former wife reduced my assets to a point that objectively, I was far from wealthy. Compared with most of the fellow students in Zürich, however, I probably appeared wealthy. Of course, I liked that feeling. I had a car and a nice apartment and could take a few impressive vacations to the Canary Islands, Greece, and the Riviera. I was also able to join a disco club at the Baur au Lac Hotel, a very expensive and prestigious hotel in Zürich where I would entertain colleagues and friends. Despite my much-reduced financial situation, I cut a pretty good figure in Zürich. That protected me from the old anxiety of feeling or appearing poor and being, as I foolishly thought, un-acceptable to others. I was, unfortunately, conditioned to think this way. Even when other students would say, presumably honestly, that money was unimportant compared with spiritual values, I was cynically skeptical. I wanted to believe what they said they believed but found it difficult to do so, despite having had what I imagined to be spiritual experiences several times in my life.

After graduating from the Jung Institute, I went to Washington, D.C., and opened a private psychoanalytic practice which I pursued for twenty-one years, until I was eighty. In Washington, I met my second wife, who was a psychotherapist and shared many of my interests. We wrote several books together.[4] While my

---

[4] My wife, Nancy Carter Pennington, and I co-authored two books: *The Guilt Cure* and *Our Creative Fingerprint*. In many important ways, she also helped me write *Guilt with a Twist* and *The Creative Soul*.

income was far less than it had been as a businessman, it was enough to support a comfortable lifestyle. Our profession and our books, lectures, and seminars gave us respectable status. While we didn't have a mansion, we had a beautiful condo on the water in Annapolis, where we spent our weekends. We were also able to have a thirty-five-foot Downeast boat custom built, and we berthed it at the marina at the condo complex. We often took friends and colleagues on the boat to various restaurants on the Chesapeake. And I was able to join the Harvard Club at The National Press Club in Washington, where I could entertain friends with meals and attend speeches by powerful and famous people that were given at the Press Club. While I was by no means wealthy, people probably thought we were pretty well off. As was the case in Zürich, that felt good and safe given my background growing up poor.

My wife and I both retired in 2012, when I was eighty, and moved to Sanibel Island, Florida, where we bought a beautiful house, thanks to the royalties from a new oil well. It wasn't as palatial or as grand as some homes on Sanibel, but it met my need to appear successful. The island itself is lovely. Unlike much of Florida, the rich vegetation had been preserved and the beaches were pristine. But Sanibel was extremely expensive, and our royalty income shrank much faster than we ever would have projected. Shale oil and gas were a relatively new phenomenon, and the decline rates associated with these wells surprised even seasoned industry veterans. We needed more wells to continue living our new lifestyle, but, while we expected new wells to be drilled, we had no control of the timing. I was worried we could reach a point at which we could no longer afford the mortgage on Sanibel. In order to reduce expenses to a level we could afford without new wells, we decided to move to Oklahoma, to the town where I had grown up. The cost of living there was much less than Sanibel. My pride kept me from telling neighbors the truth about our main reason for returning to Oklahoma. I would have been ashamed to say we couldn't afford Sanibel. It would make me feel too much as I had as a kid, when we were truly poor but tried to conceal it as much as possible. The cover story I concocted was to tell people we were moving back to Oklahoma in order to be closer to our oil and gas properties and better manage them. It embarrassed me even to tell this story, as I wasn't sure it was entirely credible. We sold our house before moving back, and I could imagine some folks might have thought if we had oil and gas money that we could have moved to Oklahoma without giving up the house in Florida. There was a partial truth in wanting to be near our oil and gas properties. It's very helpful to be there when negotiating leases as you can get more information about going lease rates from farmers in the area. And I couldn't fly there to negotiate in person as often as was needed or desirable due to my arthritic knees, which made long hours of travel and getting in and out of airports painful and difficult. There were other things we had come to dislike about Sanibel, but I wasn't comfortable talking with neighbors about them. In the winter, Sanibel was like a big resort where there was much partying, drinking, and socializing. My wife and I did not drink, nor did we like partying. It all came to feel quite shallow to us. Of course, to feel that way, I had to be totally unconscious of the shallowness of my concern with appearances and my prideful lie about the reasons for moving. Nancy never lied about this. She just kept pretty quiet on the subject and let me do most of the talking. How I appear to others is a far bigger driving force than I have ever been able to admit to myself. It isn't to say that substance is unimportant to me. But it is not as dominant in my psychic house as I once thought. Learning at Thomas Jefferson, Harvard, and the Jung Institute was important, but I am suspicious that what those credentials could do for me socially and in the job market was of equal, if not more, psychological weight.

The odd thing is that I can feel angry at others I see doing things for appearance's sake. I often feel angry at politicians and their photo ops and other rituals aimed at image-building. I can feel angry when I see ads that emphasize how products and treatments can make you look better. I often felt angry at my mother, her sisters, and my grandmother for their shallow and prideful pretensions. The anger was an informative sign, a sort of indicator of what was in my shadow. For much of my life I couldn't see that I was very much like those I criticized for their shallowness. And my guess is that, if I had been able to acknowledge my shadow needs, I would have been able to embrace them more fully and to have exploited them more effectively in terms of achieving wealth and success. For example, the inner tension and contradictions I experienced between appearances and substance kept me to a significant degree from forging and maintaining useful connections that otherwise would have been available to me both at Harvard College and Harvard Business School. The contradiction between appearance and substance pointed to a conflict between feeling that who I am and how competent I am is more important than the connections I've developed. The tensions surrounding my shadow diluted my efforts in both directions.

As for the lies I told in Sanibel in my effort to maintain appearances, I did later come to realize there probably was a reason for going to Oklahoma that had deeper meaning than the reasons I expressed. Several years before we went to Sanibel, while we still lived in D.C., I watched a beautiful Japanese movie called *Departures*. One of the most touching moments was when the hero was looking at salmon laboriously fighting upstream against the current on their way to spawn and die. They were returning to the place where they began. As the hero watched the salmon, he said, "It is so difficult to get home. I wonder if it is worth it." As he said that, I was really deeply touched. As I thought about my feelings later, I wondered what it was that aroused so much feeling in me. Does it mean concretely the physical difficulty of getting back to one's birthplace? Or is the salmon's journey symbolic of our psychological journey to our self, to God, to the unconscious, to the place where we were born psychologically? Or is it both? Is there some connection between physically and psychologically going home? Was there something in me, like the salmon, that instinctively wanted to die in the familiar place where life first started? Of course, I don't know the answer to these questions, but perhaps our move to Oklahoma was motivated in part by my desire to answer them. I also remember my Zürich analyst, John, saying to me that I'd never be depressed if I followed what interested me. "Follow the energy," he said. Going to Oklahoma literally carried out that advice. It's where my oil and gas, the energy that belongs to me, are. It is also interesting that the energy that drives our outer world comes from deep below the surface of the earth, just as we suspect that the energy that runs our bodies and our minds comes from a very deep place well below the surface of our conscious minds.

However, despite the effect on me of the movie *Departures* and my analyst's advice, I still had, dating from the day I left Ardmore with a resolve never to return, a strong resistance to living there. It took a powerful dream of a house in Ardmore to dissolve my resistance and permit me to move back. Sometimes when I am driving around Ardmore, I shake my head in wonder that I am here. After decades of negative thoughts about my birthplace, it's still hard to believe that I am actually living here. It's as if some force beyond my control brought me here. Perhaps, it's an example of something Jung said about fate and God's will: "*Mann kann freiwillig gehen oder geschleppt geworden.*"[5] One can go voluntarily or be dragged.

---

[5] I heard this at a lecture at the Jung Institute–Zürich, but I don't remember seeing it in writing.

In Oklahoma, we found a very nice house that was about a block from where I was born. The house didn't meet my need to make a bigger splash as I returned home. After all, many who knew me growing up knew I'd gone to Harvard and was a leader. They had expected me to achieve great things. For me "great things" always included making and having a lot of money and having an impressive house. Unbelievably, we only had to pay $112,500 for our new home, while we had paid $850,000 for a significantly smaller house in the Foggy Bottom neighborhood of D.C. Despite the low price, our house in Ardmore was pretty big and pretty good looking. The house had been owned by a prominent businessman who had elegantly entertained many upstanding Ardmoreites in it. Thus, despite its not being as impressive as I might ideally wish, I was not conscious at the time of feeling unbearably embarrassed or ashamed of our new house. For one thing, most of the people I grew up wanting to impress were dead. Certainly, my oldest and best friends were.

One reason for not buying a more expensive house was the ever-present vulnerability of oil and gas royalty income. Most people with the level of income we have enjoyed over the past several years normally would have more impressive houses. But oil and gas royalties are, as I indicated earlier, subject to unpredictable declines caused by falling production rates and changing prices. Typically, you need new wells to keep coming in to offset the declines. Thus far we've been lucky in that regard. New wells have continued to be drilled on our property. But it's by luck alone that this happened, because we have no control over the amount, timing, or location of the drilling. Oil companies can get loans based on oil and gas production because they do have control over when and how much to drill. For all these reasons, we pretty much have to pay cash for big ticket items like houses and cars. If we could get sizable loans, we could make a much bigger material splash, which we probably would, given the opportunity.

Shortly after we moved to Ardmore, several new oil and gas wells were completed on our property. As it turns out, from a financial standpoint, we could have easily remained in Sanibel. But it felt too risky at the time. Without being wealthy, we are quite comfortable. All of this makes the dream of a $28.5 million house in New York City suggest a kind of Icarus quality, with its absurdly soaring ambition and pretense. Something far less than a $28.5 million house should satisfy my deep yearning not to be poor or even not to appear to be poor. Something far less should also protect me from shame at my situation. It's true I was ashamed of our house growing up and always wanted to have a nice one. However, until this dream, "nice" consciously meant something far less regal than the house on East 74th Street. I never had had the conscious temerity to feel a need for or to want something so grandiose. But the Icarus in me is a quality all addicts have, the need to get higher and higher and to feel the feelings that go with it. Unfortunately, life is asymptotic. We can never quite get there, but we can exhaust and sometimes break ourselves trying.

If we think about dreams as compensatory, we could imagine a dream making up the distance between what is wished for and what, in reality, actually is. Conceptually, at least, the distance covered by this dream, which goes from a nice but inexpensive house in Oklahoma to a mansion in Manhattan, feels almost like going from zero to infinity.

This huge distance between reality and dream makes me wonder if the fear that lies somewhere deep within my unconscious is something greater than the fear of being poor, something approaching the fear of having nothing, having zero. In my circumstances, however, the fear of having nothing truly seems neurotic. It doesn't make sense. For this reason, I have come to think the dream may not be about the fear of *having* nothing, but rather the fear and humiliation of *being* nothing.

I suspect my mother did think that poor people were pretty much worthless. I heard her say such things. She would refer to one poor person or another as "nothings," as nobodies. She would also refer to my father the same way.

In my mind, I probably did equate a life with little achievement or money as both having and being nothing. It's a frightening thought. It seems to mean that what my conscious mind thought I had achieved as being significant was viewed by my unconscious mind, which brought me the grandiose dream, as virtually nothing. The dream suggests that my unconscious belief, deeply planted there by the express attitudes of my mother, is that I must be exceptionally wealthy if I am to be "something" in life, to be loved, admired, and accepted. Consciously, I knew I needed a lot to satisfy the standards of my mother. (Perhaps, "to satisfy the standards of my mother complex" is more accurate.) But until the dream, I was unaware of a possible standard planted in my unconscious mind that equated the absence of wealth with self-obliteration, far surpassing anything I had imagined.

At the core of my mother's attitudes about wealth lay, I suspect, a deep-seated belief that poor people would not be poor if they just had ambition, were hard working both in jobs and school, were responsible, had good manners, laundered and pressed and mended their clothes, mowed their lawns, and obeyed the laws. America is the land of opportunity for someone with a Calvinist work ethic. Those who don't have the ability and exert the effort to achieve much have only themselves to blame. So, under this system of belief, if I am not wealthy and do not achieve great things, I am not only a "nothing," but I also am to blame for that nothingness, bearing the guilt of that failure. It's difficult for me to understand how unconscious my mother was of the huge role that fate and luck play in shaping and determining our lives.

In a way it is a mystery how she could not see the incongruity between what she believed and her own poor condition. But the family's past wealth and her Presbyterian belief in predestination must have made her feel the family was simply in a temporary phase that destiny would correct. I suspect they felt I was part of that destiny and would help bring the family back to "glory." If the family had wealth again, my mother would love to live in a society that Jane Austin portrayed, where the purpose of poor people is essentially to serve the rich. A respectable rich person marrying a poor person was seen as scandalous, no matter how much they loved them. I'm sure they hoped I would marry someone rich who could quickly elevate my status and that of my family. Looking back, I think a couple of wealthy women really loved me. But I was too insecure to believe it. They actually had the very thing, wealth, that I thought was necessary to be loved. I suspect I was afraid I could not hold on to them if they had the money instead of me. It was too unequal for me to feel safe. I was home on vacation from Harvard once and visited John Easley, the publisher of the newspaper. He asked me why I didn't marry a certain woman whom I had dated. He said if I did, I would be a big man in Oklahoma. I was a bit shocked by his forthrightness and could only answer that I didn't know why. That's probably the right answer. I didn't want to say I wasn't in love with her, which was also true. That would have seemed mean and arrogant as well as possibly presumptuous on my part, as she might not have been in love with me, despite my thinking she was. John probably would also have wondered what love has to do with such matters. I do feel I was lucky that something kept me from marrying someone I didn't love, even if it would have technically made me rich. The truth is that they would be wealthy and not me. And I needed to be wealthy in my own right to feel safe.

Although I wasn't willing or able to take the "easy" way by marrying wealth, I now seem attracted to another kind of "easy" way. I seem to be able to imagine only the lottery providing the money I need to make my dream a reality. At my age, it is difficult to imagine actually working hard enough at something to make the kind of money I made earlier in life. I have thought of selling our mineral rights, but I think that is unlikely to produce the amount we need to fulfill the Eighteen East 74th Street dream. While the minerals support a lifestyle that would be quite satisfactory by ordinary standards, they're just not big enough to support the big dream. Nor have I been able to imagine a way to make enough money in the stock market or by some other sophisticated financial sleight of hand to support the dream. It's hard for me to believe, given the way I was earlier in life, that to get the money I need, I am focused on something I have absolutely no control over: God giving me the winning numbers.

So, daily and nightly, an endless parade of fantasies continued to assault my mind and fuel a passionate yearning for the realization of many things that seem virtually impossible for me to achieve through my own will or effort. The only paltry effort that seems to lie within my personal ability to summon up is the purchase of lottery tickets whose probability of winning feels close to zero. As more and more time passes, my dream or fantasies or efforts do not appear to have produced anything that is visibly real or concrete, so I advise myself to stop wasting my time and energy thinking about it. Unfortunately, however, my unconscious appears to be in charge of the show, and the movie rolls on no matter how much I might try to resist. My lack of power to resist is part of the entire feeling of helplessness that I am experiencing. The fantasies pull me along the way a carrot suspended before the mule pulls him forward. Something unconscious in me that I have no power over drives the relentless reels of fantasy that I am helpless to manage at all. The film that runs repeatedly appears to be totally autonomous, with a life of its own, directed by something other than my conscious self.

Fatiguing as my fantasy life is, it is, like much creative work, also fascinating and exciting. The fantasies are clearly providing images, feelings, and thoughts that have to do with things that I don't have but that my unconscious, apparently, wants. Even at the peak of my ambitions, I was truly unaware of even imagining a life like the one that would be associated with owning Eighteen East 74th Street.

So, despite all this effort to write myself into an understanding of the dream, its purpose still eludes me. The fantasies seem as impossible to incarnate now as they did when I began this piece. Certainly, there is yet no evidence whatsoever that God wants me to have the house or anything more than I now possess in the outer world. Nancy and I have bought plenty of lottery tickets whose jackpots would have been quite sufficient to buy the house. The most we have won is a measly twelve dollars.

As anyone reading my outpourings here can see, my mind remains quite ambivalent as to what the purpose of the dream and its fantasies may be. I constantly alternate as to whether it is correct to interpret the meaning as inner or outer. Sometimes, I think ambivalence is my most defining quality in all things. There's always an opposite of what my present viewpoint is that comes to mind. It's as if I need these contending opposites in order to stay conscious and to feel alive, unpleasant as the tension often is.

Because nothing substantially new appears to have presented itself in my outer life, I feel compelled to return to the thought that the meaning and purpose must be inner. And I am beginning to imagine that if the purpose is inner, it points to a process rather than an object. And I am imagining it as a psychic process rather than a psychic structure. At this point, my writing and imagining have led me to suspect that the process to which it refers is creativity, to the way humans create a life for themselves.

The flow of fantasies suggests that the way we create our lives is similar process-wise to the way we create a painting or a sculpture or a book or music. As in artistic creative processes, the dream I had provides a starting image which imagination changes into hundreds of other images, creative possibilities that eventually, after many permutations and combinations, lead the mind to an endpoint that is unknown at the beginning. The final product of the imagination can be enormously different from the starting point. A painter starts with a brush stroke and then rides his imagination through a series of additions, subtractions, minor modifications, and wholesale changes. The artist rides Pegasus but may not willfully decide where Pegasus goes. If the artist jerks on the reins, Pegasus may or may not stop, but creativity is diluted or lost, and some mechanical banality takes over. Out of the hundreds of images and scenarios that pass through an artist's imagination, only a few end up in the final product. Likewise, the parts expressed in our final creations are those that we like best, that fit together with each other, and that resonate with our soul and our self.

If we carefully watch our fantasies and observe and follow them without intent, we eventually create the life we are supposed to live. We may not like where it takes us, but we eventually arrive at a place that is a reflection of the Creator's will rather than our own.

In many ways, I don't like this conclusion, as I would very much like to have Eighteen East 74th Street in reality.

Dreams and fantasies that flow from our imagination underlie the creative process that builds and develops our lives. Dissatisfaction with the way things are stimulates our imagination to produce creative possibilities for change that cumulatively cause our lives to unfold in the particular ways they do. We don't imagine what is; we imagine what could be, what is missing in our lives rather that what we have. This ever-present and insistent dissatisfaction was called Divine Discontent by Goethe, who believed this disquieting spur is wired into us by the Creator and is the basis and fuel for all artistic production. Its purpose is to make us unhappy enough to be open to change. If we don't change, creation stops. The Creator apparently doesn't want that to happen.

Creation, and the change it produces, does not give us inner peace or serenity. It actually gives us quite the opposite. Creation depends upon a conflict between our inner masculine and feminine opposites that leads to intercourse between them, as happens after many lovers' quarrels. It produces a child, a new thing, which gives us temporary peace. Then the war begins again. If it didn't, things would stay just as they are. There would be no progress.

Nirvana probably comes when there is no desire for something more. We become reconciled to "what is" and we find peace. To surrender our dreams and fantasies of what could be and accept a state of "what is" requires a suspension of judgment. "What is" becomes neither good nor bad. It just is. I am, however, skeptical that we can suspend judgment as an act of will. I can imagine that we may reach such a state of peace when we die, but who can be sure of that? When we die, it is possible creation no longer continues for the individual, but it certainly continues for the species and in nature generally. Still, there are grounds for thinking that what is left of our bodies decomposes and changes into something else, maybe pond scum, that then begins another long process of creation, ending again in some other form, perhaps human or animal. The law of conservation of energy states that energy is never lost. The totality of life is a closed container from which no energy escapes.

It seems we pay quite a price for progress. It's a cliché that seems to be true. Creation and the suffering it entails brings change that involves destruction of the old, temporary maintenance of what is, and development of the new. Hindus represent these three states of creation as "The Three Gunas." Although some people appear to be more creative than others, I think we are all, often against our wills, creative to one degree or another.

As I have sinuously woven my way through the above analysis and commentary, with all its vacillations and contradictions, it hasn't occurred to me until just now that there actually is something that has visibly materialized in the outer world as a result of my dream. That something is the piece that I am writing at this moment. And, I must say, if this piece is its purpose, it's a monumental disappointment compared with the elevated sense of expectation that the dream originally aroused. Because the dream with all of its suggested splendor and grandeur failed to manifest in reality, I am left more dissatisfied with what is than I was before the dream. The dream left me hoping for much more. It's hard to find much satisfaction in a piece that seems to me to be at best a kind of stream of consciousness that at worst isn't even crazy enough or wild enough or absurd enough to be remotely compared with Benjy's or Quentin's rantings of sound and fury (Faulkner, 2019). The only kinship of this piece with Benjy's and Quentin's sound and fury is that it too likely signifies nothing. Even worse, such a piece would gain me no recognition in the outer world. While the inner gains it may provide are welcome, they don't provide the outer acclaim I hunger for. As I say this, I hear mother's voice. The inner stuff doesn't get seen by family, neighbors, friends, and acquaintances. She's interested in outer riches that enhance our appearance, not inner ones. She's a sore loser, so that she would indeed be disappointed if this piece, rather than a flamboyant lifestyle, is the sole result of my dream. She wants the mansion. Unfortunately, so do I.

Writing this piece is another part of the exhausting process I'm caught in. I sometimes wonder if I can survive the demands it makes on my energy. I wonder if it might, like Hemingway's old man, carry me out to sea and never bring me back.

Since what is produced by the dream in my outer world appears to be at best insignificant and at worst nothing, I can't resist trying to salvage something from it, even if it doesn't meet mother's expectations. If there is something, it certainly must be an inner thing. If the dream signifies anything, it is probably about some kind of change. The dream itself and the fantasies portray a change from my current life. And if it is about change, the change would be huge when we compare the dreamed-of life with my actual circumstances. I can now imagine it is possible that the dream is trying to open my mind to an enormous change whose endpoint, as in the case of all creative processes, is at this time utterly unknown and unknowable.

When I think of the biggest change imaginable from my present life, it would be to die. While that change would indeed seem to me to satisfy the idea of big, it would seem to be big in a downward direction, more like going from grand estates to tenements. Going from life to death does not, even symbolically, seem equivalent to going from a modest home in Oklahoma to a glittering upper east side townhouse, unless I remember biblically that my father's house has many mansions.

But a large change, whether inner or outer, could also signify something like what a sculptor may experience. He starts with a huge block of stone and gets rid of everything that isn't the endpoint toward which his creative work is leading him. He may end up with a chipmunk or a dwarf. But he may also end up with an elephant. He may also be unhappy with the result and destroy it.

I'm as ambiguous and uncertain about what transpires in the change from life to death as I am about almost everything else in life. While I am uncertain as to what the actual content of the changes might be, I am quite certain of the constancy of the process of change. Of course, this is hardly a new idea. Twenty-five hundred years ago, Heraclitus expressed the thought that nothing is permanent except change.

Still, as I reflect on my conclusion that the Eighteen East 74th Street dream and its fantasies were harbingers of my impending death, I can't avoid being skeptical. At eighty-eight, that doesn't seem like real news or much of a revelation or a prophesy worth its salt. I'd have to be a fool not to know that I don't have a lot of time left. I don't need a dream to tell me that. While death can come to anyone at any time without advance notice or warning, the probability of death being close upon me at eighty-eight is far greater than it was when I was fifty.

So, I have to reject the idea that the dream's purpose is to alert me to my impending death. As you can see, the more I write, the more my mind keeps changing as to what the meaning and purpose of the dream is. I need to be more honest and express all my thoughts as tentative, subject to change. I shouldn't say I am convinced of anything.

After all my rambling interpretations, at the moment I favor the idea that the purpose of the dream was to cause this piece to be produced. It is the only thing that has materialized in my life that I can believe emanated from the dream. It is the only change of any note that has occurred in my daily routine. The change from my usual life and its routines stands out because I now spend two to three hours per day working on this piece. Despite its demands on my energy and the exhausted state that writing it can leave me in, it feels quite meaningful and significant, even with all its vacillations and desultory meandering, its contradictions and inconsistencies, its materialism, its artlessness, its shallowness, its inflated self-centeredness, and, in places, its boastful vanity, the many ways its explorations would disappoint mother. Of course, the contradictions may be a necessary part of a piece like this, if it is to come even close to reflecting reality. This piece means much to me despite the fact that it almost certainly would mean little or nothing to my mother or to others. While my vanity would hope otherwise, deep down it knows better. Mother had to weaken in me for this piece to seem meaningful and significant to me.

The flamboyance of my dream and the fantasies it spawned stands in stark contrast to my far from grandiloquent real life. The problem for me is that in reality each day is pretty much like the day before, except for the break in routine that writing this piece has gifted me. Stealing from the bard, I can say that except for the writing:

Tomorrow, and tomorrow, and tomorrow,

Creeps in this petty pace from day to day,

To the last syllable of recorded time... (Shakespeare, 1993, 5.5.19–21.)

Without the writing, I am, at least in broad outline, pretty much a victim of my own endlessly repeating routine. I get up each morning groaning and moaning about the daily pains revealed as I slowly straighten my limbs into a full, or almost full, standing position. Owing to a broken back and a guilty memory of broken promises and broken rules of acceptable behavior that come in and out of consciousness daily, I can't now get fully upright either physically or spiritually. After this display, its sounds and gestures, I sit down for twenty minutes to do transcendental meditation, which I learned in a transcendental meditation course fifty years ago and have practiced pretty religiously twice a day ever since. Afterward, I say a short prayer, asking to be made healthy, wealthy, and wise.

Then, there's breakfast. Every day I have three dried apricots, oatmeal with yogurt, and coffee, and as I eat, I watch the news and fulminate and rage at the commentators as they spew one-sided garbage they flatter themselves by calling "news." After coffee, I take the same pills I take every other morning. Then, I put artificial tears in my eyes and clean my glasses. Ready to read, I go to my computer and review the new e-mails along with old ones I've flagged to answer. And I also rage at some of the e-mails, especially those from marketers offering frivolous products of doubtful worth, or e-mails from other crooks telling me I've won this or that lottery. Oh, if only it were true, I'd have my house on 74th Street. Then, I check my tickets for a real lottery—as opposed to the imaginary ones—offered by someone in Germany or Portugal. Next, I look at the e-mail from Oklahoma Energy Today to see if there is any news relevant to our mineral holdings. After that I look at our bank and credit accounts online to be sure there are no improper charges or invasions. At this point, I have usually become a bit fatigued, and I lie down for twenty minutes to do the breathing exercises I learned in a workshop about "mindfulness" that I attended when we lived on Sanibel.

After feeling refreshed by the breathing, I go to the Oklahoma Corporation Commission website to check applications for drilling new wells. This is a bit like checking lottery tickets. I watch intently for any proposed new drilling activity near or on our property. This activity, which often results in disappointment, has, nevertheless, a much better probability of success than the lottery, since we have several properties in areas well known from previous drilling to contain oil and gas. Then, I review the Corporation Commission's administrative law agendas to see if any meetings are scheduled on subjects that might affect our mineral rights.

Next, I usually check to see if the postman has come. With the mail, I always, before opening it and its usually disappointing contents, have an elevated expectation that I'll find something big.

Then I read the newspaper, always in the same sequence. I begin with the comics, hoping they'll dissipate some of the gloom. After the comics, I go to the obituaries. Often, they are also a bit funny and do reduce the gloom. When they are not funny, they at least spin fictions, especially when they are about people and families we know pretty well. In small towns, like the one where we live, you tend to know a lot about a lot of people.

While obituaries definitely are fiction, they are not great fiction. To begin with, obituary fiction lacks drama. Missing are many of the literary elements that might produce genuine drama: contradictions, point and counterpoint, the play of opposites, and change of pace are just a few of the missing elements. Obituaries tend to be linear and one-sided. They are almost always positive. Rarely to be seen are the dark and shadowy sides of the decedent. While obituaries aren't dramatic, they do tend to make us feel good, at least momentarily. But that may wear off as we begin to compare the glowing claims of virtue and selflessness revealed publicly by the obituary with what we know privately about ourselves and conceal on the inside. We know our inside compares very unfavorably with their outside. We have to guess what their inside was. If we assume they were really anything like their obituary claims, we feel bad about ourselves, maybe even depressed.

There is a very powerful taboo against criticizing the deceased. I'm reminded of a patient who told about his mother calling when his grandmother, his dad's mother, died. During the call, his mother talked about what a wonderful person grandmother, her mother-in-law, had been. At some point he stopped his mother and said, "Mom, stop it. You know grandmother could be a real bitch and often treated you like dirt. Are you forgetting when she called you trash to your face or accused you of being the hussy who married dad for money and security?" His mother couldn't bring herself to criticize grandmother except to add, "Well, maybe she wasn't perfect."

This man's conversation with his mother exemplifies the taboo. To speak badly of the dead feels somehow blasphemous. It violates some more-or-less unconscious, sacred boundary.

Our worry about criticism of the dead, however, is likely groundless. Obituaries have probably always tended to reflect the bright side of a two-sided moon and will probably continue to do so. Obituaries seem not only to be a good picture of how we represent ourselves when we die but also how we present ourselves while we are alive. It isn't so much that the bright side isn't entirely true; it's just that it's a half-truth. It's as unreal and inauthentic as someone who casts no shadow on a sunny day.

The obituary is the last act of presenting ourselves in a way that actually reflects the way we present ourselves all our lives. We hide the dark stuff, the dirty stuff, the outrageous stuff, the immoral stuff, the selfish stuff, the irresponsible stuff, the lazy stuff, the neglectful stuff, the cheating stuff, the cruel stuff, the sadistic stuff, the illicit stuff, the dumb stuff, the insincerity, the cowardice, the betrayals, the failures, the thoughtlessness, the insensitivity, the depressions, the unhappiness, the anxiety, the bad habits, the avarice, the stinginess, the incest, the perversions, the meanness, the hate, and the evil. This is likely a short catalogue of what is hidden on the dark sides of our reflected moons.

What we say about obituaries is also true of CVs or, as they were called in my day, resumes. They are as egregiously one-sided and positive as the obituaries. As we write our CV, we may not even be conscious of how much we are trying to fool them. Becoming conscious of such things requires some self-reflection, courage, and honesty. Most of us get at least part way there, even before the obituary. But the obituary and its positive glow shows just how powerfully deep our need is to conceal our faults and flatter ourselves.

Of course, we're never ever able to keep our shadows entirely secret from our families and close friends, if we have any who are that close. We try to hide our darkness because we aren't dummies. We know what happens if too much of who we are is too widely known or gets into the wrong hands. We hide it or we fail. If we want to be successful in conventional terms, we have to put our best foot forward, inauthentic and unreal as that picture of us may be. I say success in conventional terms because it would seem impossible in conventional society to become or remain admired and successful, if much of the dark stuff were to be revealed or exposed.

If we are lucky, we may also find a friend or spouse or partner who loves us enough to hear our stories without rejecting us. When we talk about intimacy in relationships, this is what we mean. The degree of intimacy in a relationship depends upon how much of our dark side we can share with each other without being judged or rejected by the other. While we may be able to reveal much of ourselves to such loving friends, they are still human, and, no matter how much we feel they love us, we may fear revealing some aspects of ourselves. There may be things we cannot tell them, either. For example, we just simply may not be able to tell them that we screwed a goat. With the right therapist we could probably get away with that one. But it's the hateful things we feel toward our spouses, partners, friends, and neighbors—even our therapists—that are more likely to stump us. We can share with our closest intimates stories about ourselves that are less fictional than the CVs we hand potential employers or the obituaries, written by us before dying, or by our families afterward, which are submitted to the media. Despite our deepest wishes to be honest, these stories we share with intimates will still likely contain fiction, but much less so than the stories we publicly reveal.

Society cannot stand the complete truth for the same reason individuals can't, since society is a collective reflection of them. Society also wants to be successful in its own terms. Its leaders and institutions know they must lie to be successful. They perpetuate lies like, "George Washington always told the truth." Or, "All people are created equal." Or, "Anyone can achieve the American dream." Or, "It depends on what the meaning of the word 'is' is." Or, "I'm not a crook." Or, "We're making steady progress in Vietnam." Or, "You can keep your doctors." As Churchill once said, "Truth is so precious that she should always be attended by a bodyguard of lies" (Churchill, 1952, p. 338). We don't just lie; we lie about telling lies.

Even if we would want our obituaries to tell the whole truth, we encounter serious obstacles. The truth is that it is impossible to tell the whole truth. To begin with, no one consciously knows the complete truth about himself. Even fact-laden history books can't tell the whole story. What must be left out far exceeds what can be put in. We may make our obituaries somewhat closer to reality, but in this life we never get "there." It's a limitation even science has to live with. There is always something else lying behind or beneath the last discovery. We can make the visible tip of the iceberg bigger, but we can't reveal the whole iceberg.

Neither truth nor lies monopolize the halls of goodness. Truth, however, gets a much better press and is more respectable. While truth, indeed, has much value, so do lies. If we are to grow and protect ourselves, we need to be able to practice truth and lies appropriately rather than compulsively. A compulsion to tell the truth can handicap us at times. Under any compulsion, we lose ourselves, even if it is about righteous things.

The phrase "brutal honesty" is not in our language for nothing. Truth can be mildly destructive, like learning too soon the facts about Santa. Or it can be truly destructive, as in Ibsen's play, *The Wild Duck*. This is about a blind little girl who dearly loves her doting father, whose mind is poisoned by a meddlesome friend. The friend poses as a crusader for truth, founded on the claims of an ideal where life is lived "free from all taint of deception" (Ibsen, 1961, Act 4). He knows that the girl's father is not really her father, and makes sure that this devastating fact becomes known. The truth leads to the father's rejection of the little girl, who, in her grief, kills herself. Lies and truth can be destructive as well as kind.

Many people are caught in a compulsion for honesty that may not always serve them well. Their own honesty contributes to their unhappiness and disillusionment. For example, they may hate their own jobs but can't help hearing other people talking about how much they love their work or their jobs. Hearing such positive comments may depress them or fill them with envy. Many people who they hear claiming such love for their work are not being so honest about it. It is not a good idea to walk around talking about how your job sucks. If your boss asks you how you like your job or the company, it goes much better if you tell him how much you love it. So, most people feign how they really feel. The truth is ambivalent; there is a dual reality in work just as there is in everything. Reality always contains both positive and negative elements. The problem for an honest person is that he is comparing how he feels on the inside with what wilier folks are describing on the outside.

It is admirable to be openly honest and direct, but it is naïve to expect that such honesty will always be rewarded. Though individuals often make an honest effort to bring to light negative information about institutions or events, such honesty often results in the opposite of reward. Real public honesty often gets us in trouble, albeit less trouble than what Socrates or

Jesus got into with their honesty. However, they probably were well aware that what they were saying would not turn out well for them. Contrary to what we may have been taught, there are certain kinds of honesty that can get us in more trouble than stealing. The juxtaposition of "brutal" and "honesty" are not in our vocabulary by accident. Some kinds of honesty can be brutal to others; some kinds can be brutal to ourselves. Sometimes, we can follow our honesty over the cliff without helping ourselves or anyone else.

So, if we consider making our obituaries more complete, honest, and authentic, we also need to ask what the consequences are. Who is helped and who is hurt? For the deceased, we can assume the answer is likely neutral. For surviving spouses, family members, friends, and neighbors, the effect could be devastating. It could ruin them. And think of the humiliation, embarrassment, and pain, as surviving spouses and family encounter the frowns, the bewildered looks, and the cold stares of friends, neighbors, and townspeople who read the "honest" obituary. There may be a positive benefit to some others who read the more truthful obituary and feel less negatively about themselves as they see confirmation in black and white that they are not the only ones with a lot of shit in their lives.

Maybe our obituaries should consider that there may be something more important than truth or lies. Maybe it's the potential effect on those we leave behind that is more important. Since the whole truth is never really the whole truth, why kid ourselves? And, especially, why tell it if it hurts others or humiliates, embarrasses, or debases them? We've made truth more important than kindness, sensitivity, or thoughtfulness. Perhaps more important than truth or lies is *primum non nocere*, found in the Hippocratic Oath and meaning, "First, do no harm."

All these thoughts about obituaries serve mainly to leave me quite ambivalent as to what to do or to suggest about my own obituary when I pass. I know I couldn't be as honest as I potentially might be, even if I wanted to. It would be too embarrassing and hurtful to others. At the moment, I am feeling that while it may be the coward's way out, the best way is to have no obituary at all. Any hesitation I have relates to having to pass up perhaps my last and greatest opportunity to be creative, to produce a final piece of fiction. The problem is, however, that I know in advance that it couldn't be good fiction.

Tempting as the fiction might be, I am more inclined to pass on the obituary and keep fooling them if I can. I've spent much of my life painting the best-looking portrait of myself that I could, except possibly to my analysts and most intimate friends. After all that invested effort, why intentionally throw dirt on it and besmirch that portrait at the end? I'm thinking that remaining silent may be the best way to preserve whatever fiction I had thus far created.[6]

Begging your tolerance for this detour into the fictional aspect of obituaries, I return to my daily

---

[6] Most of what is written here about obituaries and truth and lies comes from an article my wife, Nancy Pennington, and I wrote.

routine. In my typical day, after reading the obituaries, I usually eat a handful of mixed nuts. Then, I tend to scan the headlines for anything that sounds interesting. I do always look at the legal notices, as they often contain information about impending drilling activity. I end with real estate. That seems odd. Since my energy and interest is pinned on Eighteen East 74th Street, I'm not sure why I waste the time. I feel no conscious interest to move to another Ardmore house. Still, I keep looking at houses, and that tells me I must at some level feel dissatisfaction with our present house. I know it is not grand enough to meet a fanciful standard that lies deep within my unconscious, as borne out by my dreams. Bearing in mind my dreams as well as my mother's and grandmother's pretensions, it feels to me that satisfying the standard harbored by my unconscious for what is "grand" means something almost unimaginably grand, like Eighteen East 74th Street. Apparently, what passes for grand in me cannot even be found in Ardmore.

When I read the Ardmore real estate section, I usually notice some fantasies rolling in, but they don't come close to the rapturous splendor or proliferating imagery of those spawned by Eighteen East 74th Street. One of these much less spectacular real estate fantasies arose when I noted in the paper that 1600 Stanley Street, SW, in Ardmore had come up for sale. It, too, is a magnificent house. It would be incredible if it were located in Manhattan, but it is not a style found there. The style would probably fit better on Long Island or perhaps the Hamptons.

I regarded it as one of Ardmore's most impressive mansions when I was growing up. It's in a very upscale neighborhood, next door to where John Easley, the original publisher of *The Ardmoreite*, lived, and across the street from another mansion, the house that once belonged to Ward Merrick, who was a rich Ardmore oil man. It's near the former home of the Riesens as well as the Coes's house, which also just came up for sale. To one degree or another, my fantasy life feeds on houses and the thought of living in an impressive one. The fantasies definitely compensate for the shame I felt about the unimpressive house I actually lived in.

I don't remember the name of the people who owned 1600 Stanley when I was young. They were not socialites, and their name was not so widely known as Easley, Merrick, Coe, and Riesen. The house at 1600 Stanley just looks really nice. It is two-story brick, trimmed in stone, with a *porte cochère*. There is a swimming pool, an outdoor kitchen and grill, and a separate studio with bath. Unlike most houses in Ardmore, it has a basement with a movie screen and theater seating. When I read about the movie seating, I began to imagine forming a Jungian group to watch movies and discuss dreams. That would definitely give Nancy and me something to do that could be interesting. I'm surprised energy has arisen for Jungian stuff, as I had lost almost all interest while I was having all the surgery and recovering from it.

In my fantasies I am also feeling a rush when I imagine people seeing us at 1600 Stanley. While it's a high, it is nothing compared with the one triggered by imagining us living in Eighteen East 74th. Both rushes feel good, but one is more like heroin and the other like wine or at best a martini. Compared with Eighteen East 74th Street, my Ardmore fantasies have shrunk considerably in scale. Downscale as 1600 Stanley may be, I still imagine the admiring glances resulting from my ownership. Absent from these fantasies are the NetJets, a chef, and an administrative assistant. Also gone are fantasies of lavish entertainment.

These more modest fantasies don't require winning the lottery to be satisfied. They do require a big increase in royalty income. I can imagine a sufficient income in two to three years, but I assume the house will be sold before that to some wealthy doctor or lawyer. In addition, the inside of 1600 Stanley has nothing of the taste and elegance of Eighteen East 74th. The outside is nice, but we would have to do a lot to the inside to make it fit our tastes and reach at least some hint of grandeur.

With all my dreams and fantasies about grand houses, I'm coming to suspect that houses, more than any other objects or images, must for me somehow be the most accurate and powerful symbol of success and wealth. Somewhere, very deep within, I must feel that my house makes a statement about who I am more than anything else. I have had dreams in the past of very famous, very successful people, so they may also symbolize the same thing in my psyche. But the most powerful and persistent dreams and fantasies have been about houses. It's true that growing up I was very ashamed of my house, particularly the inside. That may also be true of myself. I'm more ashamed of the inside than the outside and less willing to reveal the inside as well.

My obsession with houses is probably a good example of Freud's use of the term "cathexis." In psychoanalysis, "cathexis" is defined as the process of investment of mental or emotional energy in a person, object, or idea. Even my fantasies about winning the lottery or becoming really rich on oil are at bottom about houses. It's as if I feel there is no point in being wealthy unless I can show it. And showing it starts with the house. Other things, like furniture, art, cars, clothes, NetJets subscriptions, travel, and similar acquisitions, also add to the statement that I wish to make, but it starts with the house. As I wrote earlier, however, the attainment of great wealth and success as expressed by houses, famous people, and so on, are but the means to a more important end: possessing mother's love, as evidenced by "that look." Actually, there is still something behind "that look" that represents our deepest, truest goal. It's the incomparably exquisite feeling that it produces.

Growing up, my house looked okay from the outside, but was awful on the inside. That combination makes me want to keep people out, so that they're unable to see my inside. I have had the experience of seeing a house that looked quite modest, even off-putting, on the outside but that was quite lovely and impressive on the inside. I remember particularly a house in DC that was just a block away from our Georgetown house. It was for sale, and there was an open house. The outside was a kind of faded gray that definitely needed a paint job. The minute I walked in the door the view was breathtaking. Rich and elegant furnishings, drapes and rugs, paintings, some by known artists, beautifully framed and presented, some fine statuary, everything in good taste, at least in my eyes. Then, I walked out the back door into a large walled English garden with a sparkling swimming pool. Behind that was a lovely guest cottage. The contrast between inside and outside was the opposite of my house in Ardmore. And I came to like the idea of a house like that where the inside is a huge upside surprise. It's like revealing your warts and darkness and hiding your beauty and light. It's the opposite of what we do in our obituaries, CVs, and other statements of ourselves.

The home at Eighteen East 74th Street is beautiful and elegant both on the inside and the outside. When one sees the façade of Eighteen East 74th Street, one would be surprised to find anything less than impressive on the inside. There are no surprises. The owners' best foot is forward wherever you look. In a way, this house symbolizes an ideal that is unattainable to the vast majority of us. But I suspect it is a metaphor for the ideal I unconsciously aspire to myself, unattainable as it might be.

Last night I had a dream in which only the words: "Joshua Means" appeared. It felt a bit like my Eighteen East 74th Street dream in which only a few words appeared. It also feels related to the Eighteen East 74th dream in another way. I googled, "What does Joshua mean?" and found that the Hebrew name, Joshua, means "Jehovah is generous" and "Jehovah saves." Joshua succeeded Moses as the leader of the Israelites for their journey to the Promised Land. It made me wonder if Eighteen East 74th might symbolize for me an inner construct that is my inner equivalent to the Promised Land. They both sound like glorious, uplifting, enchanted places. But it's the incredible *feeling* we imagine getting from the Promised Land, or Eighteen East 74th, that makes us want to possess it as Joshua and the Israelites did. It is the *feeling* that flows from "that look" that makes us want to possess it, as well. In life we find numerous archetypes and ideas that are close equivalents to The Promised Land: for example, there's heaven and nirvana. And we have a lot of experiences that are earthly surrogates for these ideas, that seem heavenly and often are described as such. They are more down-to-earth experiences that momentarily make us feel we are in heaven or have reached the Promised Land: falling in love, inebriation with alcohol or drugs, winning at cards, winning the lottery, great achievements, transcendence in meditation or prayer, promotions, getting straight A's. There are many others: dragging Main in our new red Cadillac, exquisite food, sex (especially with someone long yearned for), orgasm, striking oil, acceptance letters from publishers, winning the nomination, becoming President, a huge transformative insight—spiritually, scientifically, or artistically—a Pulitzer Prize, a Nobel Prize and, of course, "that look." Events like these can all momentarily take us to the Promised Land or, at least, the heavenly feeling associated with it. In the movie, *Nebraska*, Bruce Dern believes he's won a million dollars, but when asked what he wanted to use it for, he says, "A new pickup." Driving the truck down Main Street in the town where he was born was the nirvana moment for him. For me, it's entering Eighteen East 74th.

If Eighteen East 74th stands for heaven or the Promised Land, it is also a place I may never reach, depending upon whether I have Moses' experience or Joshua's. As we recall, Moses was allowed to see the Promised Land, but he couldn't set foot in it. The Moses experience is what many of us frequently face in life. It is the asymptotic experience, where we feel we approach but never get to where we ultimately want to go. We get closer and closer but never arrive. It's the dynamic of life that makes us seekers, keeps us looking for something we never find. We may have to die to actually get there.

The search for the Promised Land is a sad—but still very promising—picture that postpones our reaching our destination, unless by some great good fortune Joshua should appear and lead us there. Living life by the Moses experience is to be guided by the rules, the law. A life so guided may also end in regret. I can at least imagine that Moses felt regret at not reaching the place for which he yearned. I know I, too, have had regrets but, of course, I broke "the law" multiple times.

Living life by the Joshua experience is to be guided by the spirit. Many Jungians feel the spirit is an idea that is similar in many ways to the self. Living life "by the rules" is somewhat more straightforward and comprehensible. It's an easier way to understand what to choose and what to do. Living life by the spirit depends a lot more on nuance, on intuition. It may consider dreams and fantasies as a source of guidance. It's more difficult to understand and fraught with much more uncertainty. There are fewer traffic lights, fewer guideposts and warning buoys. Living life by the spirit demands living with a huge tolerance for ambiguity.

In my early adult life, I was hardly living by the spirit. I was trying to reach the Promised Land not symbolically, but literally. I spent my life trying to make the outside look as good as I could make it. I invested a tremendous amount of energy in my education at Thomas Jefferson School, Harvard, and the Jung Institute. They were all part of the drive to be and look successful. All along the way, I tried to have the most impressive house I could afford. I suspect I always spent a larger percentage of my income on places to live than most people. Even in Switzerland, where I had to be careful with money, I had a lovely apartment next to a beautiful park in Zollikon. In D.C. I got a condo on the water in Annapolis and eventually rented an old but classical house in Georgetown. An example of how emotional I am about the house I live in and how it appears to others is a comment made by a Jungian friend about our house in Georgetown. It was really a charming, very expensive old Georgetown house with a great address. Our friend was a wealthy woman who was training to become a Jungian analyst. When she asked me my address one day and I told her, she said, "Oh, that's in Burleith, isn't it?" Burleith is definitely a step down from Georgetown and was located several blocks north of us. Her comment about Burleith stung so deeply that I have remembered her comment all these years. It felt like a great put-down and definitely hurt after all the struggle to get into a prestigious house in a prestigious neighborhood. The woman had lived in D.C. for thirty years, and she damned well knew the address was not in Burleith.

Later, I bought a house in another prestigious neighborhood, Foggy Bottom, which was a tremendous stretch financially. In retrospect, I think I felt unconsciously that I had to buy this house not only to look good in the eyes of friends and colleagues but also to hold on to Nancy. She really loved the place. Consciously and objectively, I know this thought is "my shit," as I am very sure Nancy loved me long before I had the Annapolis condo or the Georgetown and Foggy Bottom houses. She loves me despite knowing more about my dark stuff than anyone else in this world. She is the love of my life. Still, I was helplessly unable to keep from projecting on to Nancy a viewpoint that belonged to my mother. I was seventy-four years old at the time and still unavoidably feeling the same way I did with Jacqueline Chesser when I was eight or nine years old, that I wouldn't be loved if I couldn't be wealthy and provide a woman with the good things of life. That feeling also belonged to mother and not Jacqueline. My mother's message got to me, and I haven't to this day been able to entirely rid myself of the hold it has on me. While psychoanalysis and other work to become more conscious may have helped weaken its hold, nothing yet has removed it.

I can feel even today at eighty-eight some disappointment and dissatisfaction with the house we have. It is the best we could do in our financial circumstances and the inability to use fluctuating oil royalties to get loans. I try to make the best of it that I can. We spent quite a lot of money on landscaping to make our front yard look really beautiful. And when people ask me where I live, I don't first give the address but say we bought Millard Ingram's house. Millard was a prominent Ardmore businessman. Many people know him or his daughters and have actually been in the house. They usually light up when I say that, if they, in fact, knew Millard and his wife. He lived there for forty years before going to a nursing home. That's when we bought it. The house is still pretty nice, inside and out, but it is next to a strip mall and the parking lot of Payless Shoe Store. You can see a Love's gas station and convenience store from our front door. This setting really takes away from what could otherwise be a fairly prestigious house. That's likely why we got it for $112,500, which was all we could afford at the time. While we could easily afford a much more expensive house now, we can't get a mortgage because of the problem of using royalty income as a basis for loans. Thus, we would have to save up enough cash to buy whatever we wanted. I am not content with our house and dream grandiose dreams about spectacular houses. The degree of powerlessness to get a more prestigious house that I feel is reflected in the huge gap between my actual house and the one I dream of.

To the extent that houses are a metaphor of myself, neither my inside nor my outside live up to my dreams. Everyone sees the outside of our house, but few see the inside. We're pretty reclusive, and, although the inside looks okay, it, like the outside, is a disappointment to me. We have done some work on the inside, but it is not something yet that I can feel really proud of. And the bidet dream I had earlier suggests that it is the inside, the part that is not visible, like the genitals, that really needs to be cleaned up.

I may not be completely fair to myself when I say that I have so cathected the house and how its appearance reflects me that it has become the most important thing to me. During the past year Nancy and I have spent $80 thousand or more on health and dental issues. We could have practically rebuilt our house for that or made a huge down payment on another home. Or we could have bought a fancy car. But we opted to spend it on health instead. But when I am honest, that still had to do at least partly with appearances. I had heart surgery and two knee replacement operations in New York City at the Hospital for Special Surgery and Cornell University Medical Center. We had to make five roundtrip flights from Dallas to New York and spend seventy-five days at the very expensive Helmsley Medical Tower in order to get all of this accomplished. Of course, we flew first class. It's a good story that I like because it smells of money and calms my anxiety about appearing not to have it.

When I read the paragraph I just wrote, I am consciously quite aware of how pathetic and neurotic it sounds. I even feel some compassion for myself and can easily understand why it would feel humiliating and probably dumb to ever admit this publicly. I can own up to this "shit" with Nancy, and that feels safe enough, because amazingly, despite all my paranoia, I trust that she loves me, even knowing this kind of childishly pathetic stuff about me. Just as I write this, I am reminded of another silly incident in which I felt this need to appear to have money. Soon after I moved back to Ardmore, I was riding my adult recumbent trike near the house and saw three neighbors talking. One was Rick, the retired Presbyterian minister who had presided for years over the church I grew up in under the stern hands of my mother and grandmother. Another was the current mayor of Ardmore, Doug, and Bob, a retired rancher. I stopped to talk and during the conversation one of them mentioned Mike Mordy's name. Mike is an Ardmore attorney. The minute I heard the name Mordy I involuntarily, despite knowing at the very moment I was saying it, just how pretentiously vain, shallow, and needless the comments were, launched into a story about him. I told them I had heard Mordy's name when I was attending the National Association of Royalty Owners meeting in Pittsburgh. Of course, just telling them that part let them know I owned mineral rights. I went on to say that Lin Willers, an officer of the association and head of Wells Fargo's minerals department, when he learned I was from Ardmore, mentioned to me that if I ever needed a great attorney there is one in Ardmore named Mike Mordy. Lin said he knew that because Mordy had once been the attorney on the opposing side of Wells Fargo and had eaten their lunch. I recounted all of this to the neighbors. I could have bitten my tongue off as

I heard myself saying this as I knew how needlessly pretentious this would sound. The wise thing would have been to keep quiet. But I just can't resist impulses that make me appear to have money even while knowing how tenuous our money is. Despite several years of really good income from royalties, we have not saved much. Oil and gas income always hangs by a slender thread. Production declines can be rapid, as can price declines. I think the price of oil is more volatile than the stock market. So, I'm aware I can be talking one day in a way that suggests we are well off only to be down to very modest income in a short period if our luck doesn't continue. But despite my conscious knowledge of how stupid all of this is, I simply can't stop myself. I'm reminded of our old lab, Tilly. Whenever we left the house without her, she would go into the living room and shit in the middle of our beautiful carpet. Each time she did that we would roll up a newspaper and beat her pretty hard. It really scared Tilly. She knew she had done something bad, but she kept doing it. Finally, we felt sorry for Tilly and took her with us wherever we went. I can even feel sorry for myself for repeated incidents that are similar to the conversation I just reported with my neighbors. Even if I were actually poor again, I think I would behave like Tilly. I just can't stop myself from periodically showing my rear in a pretentious way. The funny thing is that I do have a kind of faith that God will take care of me as he has all these years. But I also know how pretentious that sounds as I make myself out to be special. Even when I am saying that about God I am aware that my feeling about my relationship to God is also a pretty slender reed to hold on to. But I do. And I have for a long time. The slender part belongs to me. The relationship part belongs to my need to feel special. I also think it has something to do with my early exposure to talk in my house about our Presbyterian predestination and how that concept applied to us. And by the way, the bike I was riding when I encountered my neighbors is an adult recumbent trike, a three-wheeler. Nancy and I both own one and the bikes cut a pretty good figure and suggest something that—well, you know what.

To return now to my otherwise predictable daily routine that has been significantly altered only by time and effort spent on this piece, I finish off the morning by checking out e-mails again.

Now it's time for lunch. It is almost as predictable as breakfast. I always have soup, but I have a choice of three different ones: navy bean, split pea, and chicken noodle. I always have apple sauce and a piece of bread. My beverages are lemon ginger tea and water to take the same noon pills that I take daily. While eating lunch, I watch the news, as I do at breakfast, and that usually makes me fulminate some more.

After lunch, I lie down for twenty to forty minutes. Sometimes I drop off to sleep. Then, I get up and return to my computer. I check the Oklahoma Corporation website again to see if there are any new developments. Afterwards, I do three Duo Lingo and one Rosetta Stone French chapters. Then, I read a few stories in *Le Figaro*.

Now it's time for exercise. Every day I go either to the health club or for a walk. Walking is new for me since for eight years before my knee replacement surgery, it was too painful to walk more than a few feet at a time. Now I've built up to forty-five-minute walks and have a goal to reach an hour. Before going to the health club, I drink an Ensure to give me extra energy. I drive the same route to the health club each day: West Broadway to Commerce, north on Commerce to 15th. I'd be an easy target for an assassin but so far so good. I talked with a business man in El Salvador years ago and he said he took a new route to work every day. They still shot him.

On the way home from the health club, I stop by Walgreens, if there are any prescriptions to pick up. Every other day I stop by McDonald's for a plain sundae, which I take home and put in the refrigerator for an after-dinner treat. At home I do some back stretches and tai chi. I check my computer again for any relevant, new oil and gas information on the Corporation Commission website. I also check e-mails. Then, I meditate again for twenty minutes and say another short prayer: heal my body and mind and soul. Again, before dinner I check e-mail, particularly Robert Winslow's daily drilling permit and completion reports.

Then, there's dinner. This does vary somewhat from day to day. But there are seven meals that are mainstays: curried chicken, grilled salmon, scallops, spaghetti with turkey meatballs, chicken meatloaf, a kind of chef's salad, baked cod. Usually we have mashed or sweet potatoes with the main course, a mixed salad, and another serving of apple sauce. I only have water with dinner, using it to take my evening pills. During dinner we watch a Netflix movie or a series like *Madam Secretary, Pride and Prejudice, Sneaky Pete, House of Cards, Breaking Bad,* or something similar. At a break, I either eat my sundae or some popcorn. Around eleven I usually go to bed after setting the air-conditioning to sixty-seven degrees and cleaning my teeth. I remember Arianna Huffington writing something about sixty-seven degrees being optimal for sleep. I slip the CPAP mask on, say another prayer, and do my breathing exercise until I fall asleep. So, that's about it. That's pretty much my program, and I maintain this routine daily. Oh, I forgot to mention having to go to the toilet day and night far more often than most people owing to my enlarged prostate.

As I review what I have written, I become increasingly aware of its banality, its egotism, its vain boasting, its incoherence, its inconclusiveness. Unfortunately, despite its boastfulness, I've had to reveal a lot that touches my shallow materialism. I imagine it is not something that would be even mildly interesting to anyone other than me or, perhaps, Nancy. Certainly, I would be quite embarrassed, if not humiliated, for others to read it, even in this much diluted version showing only parts of who I am. Since this piece reveals only the tip of my giant shadow, I can only imagine the impact of revealing the whole thing, even if I could. If I'm not foolish enough to show this shortened version to others, it's hard to imagine revealing the complete version. I haven't even written the complete version. I wouldn't even want Nancy to see that, loving and forgiving as she is. The complete version would likely cause friends to say they understand why I have moved around so much: leaving one place for another before I got found out or at worst moving to stay one step ahead of the bailiff.

Revealing our shadow is a very scary thing to do and does have its dangers. I did a lot of this in therapy, where I felt reasonably safe revealing myself, with the exception of negative thoughts about my therapists. I also wrote my shadow stuff down in AA and in my journaling over the years. Of course, I kept these jottings under lock and key. So I know a good bit about my dark side despite the fact that the writing I have revealed thus far reflected mostly the bright side. By writing for my eyes only and keeping it hidden, I could hope that knowing as much of my own shadow as possible would be sufficient self-revelation to bring some serenity and peace. That hope has not materialized, at least not yet.

I will go so far as to say openly that I violated more or less all the ten commandments, except the one about murder. I won't go into detail but will say that one experience about stealing made me realize that it is probable that everyone is a thief; it's just a question of degree. That thought was somewhat comforting, kind of like Clint Eastwood's observation in the movie *Unforgiven* that there are only two kinds of people: the caught and the uncaught. When I was in business, my secretary commented that taking legal pads, pencils, or even paper clips home was stealing. I did that all the time without thinking about it or being the least bit conscious that I was stealing. But technically she was right. It's company property. I suspect there are few people who don't cheat this way or round the numbers in their expense accounts, if not outright make false statements.

I am certainly a liar, but I comfort myself by thinking that almost everyone else is, too, again more or less. But as I wrote earlier, lying appears to me to be both the wise and the kind thing to do in some circumstances. I truly believe this, and that thought probably keeps some feelings of guilt at bay. I've written a lot about honesty elsewhere and often cite the Ibsen story of *The Wild Duck* to support my view. There are many small ways that people lie, besides their CVs and obituaries. We often falsify our feelings by saying we feel one way when in truth we don't. In certain circumstances we may deny that we feel angry, unhappy, disappointed, hurt, or jealous. For example, if we speak in an angry tone to someone and they ask us if we are mad at them, often we say something like, "No, I have no reason to be mad at you." If someone asks us how we are, we normally don't burden them with how we actually feel, even if we are unhappy and depressed. If you ask a Swiss person how he is, he is likely to reply, *Gestern ging es gut aber heute ist noch nicht fertig.* "Yesterday went well, but today is not yet finished." This reply hedges the bet enough not to be a total lie.

I am also guilty of much profanity and taking God's name in vain. I do know there is a God of some kind that is responsible for this incredible created world. I am quite aware of how dependent I am upon him/her/it. But I also believe God has a dark side and is responsible for as much wonderful as awful stuff in our lives and life in general; awful, at least, as seen through our ego's eyes. Who brings the tornadoes, hurricanes, diseases, and so on? I pray a lot but know God only answers and does what he wants and wills. But when I am hurting, I know God is often the only one who could possibly help. So, I ask for help even knowing I may not get it. It's the same as it was with parents when we were children. Who else was there to cry out to for help? But they didn't always bring it. Of course, I know that if God gave me everything I asked for or wanted that it would be the same as my being God. I am pretty sure that I have an unconscious wish to be God. It's a wish that compensates my often total sense of helplessness and impotence. Of course, as crazy as I have been at times in my life, I've never been crazy enough to consciously think I was God. Not yet, at least.

I don't make false idols and worship them but, technically, I probably do violate this commandment by making gods of money, prestige, and success. And as I've said, I probably unconsciously want to be God.

I can also admit to a lot of betrayals. I betrayed my mother, my best friend, and a couple of bosses.

While I do lie, I'm not sure I have given false evidence against anyone. I probably have but can't come up with an example.

I'm very guilty of the envy commandment. I envy people with lots of money, those who are extremely successful, those who appear to be good and to have lived model lives. I envy brilliant people and wish I were brilliant. I'm smart, but not smart enough to be able to salve my envy. Of course, I know this won't change. I do a lot to try to appear smart, like Julien

Sorel in Stendhal's *The Red and the Black,* just as I do a lot to try to appear successful and well off. I probably value appearing smart because it got "that look" from mother. Like Julien Sorel, a country boy like me who tried to make it big in the city, I often use quotes and some linguistic ability to make me look smart and seem knowledgeable and cultured. I keep a few choice Shakespeare quotes handy, like Hamlet's soliloquy. We had to memorize a lot of passages when I was at Thomas Jefferson School. And I keep these passages in mind by reviewing them from time to time so that I can appear to spontaneously recite them from ancient memory. I also remember singing *La Marseillaise* in French to a group at a party in Zürich. As a result of their compliments, I feel sure they thought I was fluent in French. My French is pretty good, but not that good. I can also belt out a few Latin phrases when it seems appropriate. *Arma virumque cano.* "I sing of arms and the man," the opening lines of the *Aeneid*. Those phrases probably contribute some to an impression of a retained classical linguistic ability, but the truth is that these phrases are all that have survived from my original knowledge of Latin, despite having passed the Latin entrance exams for Harvard. I was too pre-occupied with trying to make money and be successful to continue the work and study necessary to genuinely become what I was trying to project. It's hard to find a convincing way to appear rich and successful (or genuinely cultured and scholarly) if you aren't. Unfortunately for my pretentious ego, while I have a very comfortable life, I am not wealthy or successful in terms that satisfy the inner standard that

I believed triggered "that look." At least, it feels that way.

Jealousy is a feeling closely related to envy. From very early in my life, jealousy was palpably and uncontrollably present within. It was present in my relationship to my mother and brother. It tainted and disturbed all my romantic relationships, and affected my feelings toward colleagues, especially in the highly competitive world of business. I needed to be "the one." Outwardly, I concealed my competitiveness and jealousy as best I could, knowing it is a quality that can make others wary, uneasy, and even angry, just as I had those feelings when I saw competitiveness and jealousy in others. But despite my efforts to conceal my jealousy and competitiveness, I am certain it leaked through the seams of my being.

While I was finishing this manuscript, Nancy and I spent a month in Paris. There we were walking through the Pompidou Centre and noticed a painting called *Mon Envie: D'Etre le Seul.* "My wish: to be the only one." It struck my wife and me at the same moment. We both immediately sensed that it captured a dominant thread that is woven through my life and way of being in the world.

I am aware of another quality that doesn't violate any commandments *per se* but does trespass norms of the respectable thought and behavior approved by most people. In a most fundamental way, I am extremely irresponsible. I don't think I am noticeably irresponsible in conventional ways. I pay my bills and taxes. I don't keep people waiting or miss important appointments. I vote and don't break the law except in very small ways. No, I feel irresponsible in a more profound and puzzling way. I don't feel responsible for who I am or who I have become. I feel the person that I am more or less just "happened" as a result of some kind of early wiring or an inner force that dominated my thoughts, feelings, and behavior. I don't feel responsible for how I think or act or feel. Of course, a judge and most others would laugh at that defense, if I had been hauled into court for having broken the law. Still, I suppose they can't jail me for not *feeling* responsible for who I am.

Coming to believe late in life that my unconscious essentially runs my show, retrospectively suspecting it has always been so but that the ego was blind to it (and probably needed to be blind to it), has led me to a view about our power of choice that seems related to something Jung wrote about psychic energy and willpower. He wrote that willpower is the amount of psychic energy the self makes available to the ego. It feels to me that Jung is saying that we basically can only do what the self agrees with. If the self disagrees with our wish or choice, we don't get the energy to carry it out. I suspect that his idea at least partially explains depression as a withdrawal or the self's withholding of psychic energy we wish to use but can't. It is possible the ego may be so out of line with the self that it doesn't even have the energy to wish. Before I leave this point, however, I need to emphasize that I am quite aware that as long as anyone's goal is to be successful, it is important that they feel they can make choices, that they are responsible for those choices, and that the choices, along with thought and effort, actually shape outcomes. It's important to feel this way, even if it may not be true. In the first half of life, at the least, I suspect we are wired to believe this is true. As I've thought about things late in life, once I became certain that I did not and could not choose the dreams that had had such a powerful influence on my life, it didn't seem like a huge leap to suspect the same to be true of my thoughts and feelings. They seem no more intentional than my breathing. Thinking, breathing, and feeling are subject to momentary conscious control. But one measure of our ultimate lack of control is our inability to stop these things for longer than a brief interval.

If you are reading my book, it is surely obvious to you that my views about our power of choice in life are out of the mainstream of psychological thought. My view is also different from the way most laymen think about it. I also suspect many reading this book would think I am not only irresponsible but also quite narcissistic. In the case of irresponsibility, I'm not very guilty by standard definitions. But I am guilty in the much deeper sense of not *feeling* responsible for who I have become. And I am certainly narcissistic, not in the clinical sense, but as defined by Norman Mailer who, as noted earlier, believed it was an over-simplification to think of narcissism as self-love (Mailer, 1976). In Mailer's view, narcissism has fundamentally to do with a relationship to one's self, an inner dialogue between an observer and other parts of himself where the observer self is absorbed in studying the other self (Mailer, 1976). For many years now, I have actually experienced myself as constantly observing myself and wondering why I thought what I did, felt the way I did, or did what I did. Becoming aware that I am observing myself didn't occur until the second half of life when failures of one kind or another caused me to reflect on myself. Before that, I pretty much felt that there was just one me, and it was all up to me. After the failures, I noticed there was more than one me. I've mentioned some of those failures, but probably the one with the most impact on my life was becoming aware that I was an alcoholic. That insight felt as if it were a spiritual experience and the beginning of my observing myself and knowing I was observing myself. I also, like Mailer, came to believe that the process of one self looking at another self in a kind of inner dialogue contributed significantly to my creativity, the writing which has produced this book and four others.

At a distance now from my younger years, I have a very different sense of who I am. And that keeps changing as more dreams and insights occur. It can't be denied, however, that like Narcissus I am fascinated by myself and spend a lot of time and energy looking at myself. I'm attracted to anything I suspect could be a faithful psychic mirror. But I can tell you that I certainly do not love all I see or necessarily find it beautiful.

Most importantly, perhaps, discovering that there was more than one *me* basically dashed my wish to be the only one, *le seul*. That wish wasn't ruined by my brother, some male friend taking my girlfriend, or another belittling event; I dashed it myself, internally. Ultimately, the realization that I was not one but many was liberating, but it certainly didn't feel that way at first. Initially, it was a very depressing experience: after decades of struggle, a sudden epiphany laying to waste too many proud accomplishments, all strived for in order to be the most successful, the most accomplished, the one.

My sense of having many selves may have come clear to me all at once, but it had been building for many years, since midlife. Increasingly since midlife I have been able to observe and become more conscious of my thoughts, feelings, and behavior, but as I became more conscious of them, I stopped experiencing them as a result of clear personal choice. Generally, I don't feel I am the author of my thoughts. I don't even feel as though I am the author of what I am writing here. It feels as though I am the scribe.

When I find myself valuing my writing as an inner experience, that increases my consciousness of who I am. I feel that experiential sort of writing as coming not from mother, but from an entity inside me, someone other than the "me" that I think of myself as being. I experience my thoughts and feelings more as I do my breathing and its regulation by the autonomic nervous system. It feels as if someone or something other than "I" does the breathing for me. And I could throw aches and pains into this whole mix. I definitely don't feel responsible for them. They seem to come the same way my breathing, thoughts, and feelings come. This perception extends to retrospection. When I look back on my life, I feel an inability to have done otherwise. I don't think I had the power to change the way it went. I certainly wasn't powerless to do things;

rather, I was powerless to decide *what* to do. I had a lot of energy, but I wasn't directing it.

In truth, I question whether we are capable of making conscious choices. Our egos, especially our superegos, believe that we make conscious choices and that we are responsible for what we choose. The collective consciousness certainly agrees with that assessment. But just because the collective consciousness and our individual egos have faith in our logic and reason doesn't make them our governing faculties. Much as our heartbeats and breath are controlled by unconscious factors, there are grounds for inferring that the unconscious runs our minds and feelings as well.

This feeling of not being responsible for my thoughts, feelings, choices, and behavior didn't come to me until late in life, well into the second half of it, when I had the following dream:

I am at an amateur play watching the stage. There are two stark figures. The Queen/Mother is on the left on a simple throne. She has on a gown with plain and simple lines. The King/Son is on the right, also on a simple throne. The mother reads from a page and the son repeats it. The lines are poetic and nice but not original. They are both saying lines written by someone else.

The dream shook me and caused me to question much that I had believed about myself until then. For most of my life, until this dream and other psychic experiences changed my way of looking at myself, I did have the feeling that I was in charge of myself and that my thoughts and feelings belonged to me. I especially felt that way about my successes. But I also felt that way about most of my failures, especially my alcoholism. The spiritual experience that led to my recovery from alcoholism along with the dream recounted above awakened me to the idea that something bigger than myself was at work in me, and that the person I thought I was was subordinate to that larger thing.

As I look back, I definitely would have changed some things if I had been my own boss. But I wasn't the CEO; at least I didn't feel as if I was. I was the executive vice president who carried out the CEO's wishes. I'm still not sure who the CEO of my life is. Sometimes, when I analyze it, it can feel like mother. Since mother was my first image of God, I might also think God was running the show. But that's probably an even more grandiose idea than living at Eighteen East 74th Street. In any event, it's hard to believe God was running the show, as I feel sure he would have done a much better job. On the other hand, who am I to judge? Maybe I'm what I'm supposed to be, whether I like it or not? Maybe a flawed human is as much what he is supposed to be as a bent and crooked oak is what it is supposed to be? I like this story. Since the existence or non-existence of God and his ways are unprovable, why not pick the story we like? One reason I like this story is that it relieves me of a huge burden of guilt. I know my view sounds pretty infantile to reasonable people. But what can a momma's boy say?

Clearly, the conventional and legal view is that I am responsible for myself, particularly what I say and do, including what I write. Earlier in life I thought the conventional view was, indeed, correct. Later in life that view changed, but it is a new view acquired by looking through a lot of silt that disturbed the water I was glancing into. I had to draw inferences from a murky bunch of thoughts, feelings, fantasies, and images. While I'm not absolutely certain of the truth of the view that evolved, it is the one I believe to be true. I have come to think that I needed to have the earlier view but also needed to have the later one. Both are important to the way I have turned out.

Since I know I am conventionally and legally responsible for myself in the outer world, I am, perhaps wisely, afraid to put all my known flaws and trespasses in writing and publish them. I remember saying to Nancy that I wasn't sure whether it would be courageous or foolhardy to publish this piece. Maybe foolhardy is a double entendre. My middle name is Hardy. While thinking I was fooling others, I might just be fooling myself. The orange peel is also a double entendre. I have probably thought of it as analogous to my persona, whose purpose is to keep others from seeing what's inside me. But the peel may also make it more difficult for me to see what is inside of me. I suspect that I could be as afraid to become aware of some of my deeper unconscious flaws and trespasses as I would be to reveal to others the ones I know. There's even the question of whether some of the deeper stuff is worth knowing or is too risky to know. I suspect dangers can lurk there. So far something has protected me from potential psychic threats. I've been lucky. My guess is that some of the psychic contents are so horrible, by my ego's standards, that even I couldn't bear to know them, unless the impact were to be mitigated by being able to see in reflection, viewing myself in the magic mirror I referred to earlier that permits us to become aware of the horrible, odious, repugnant, reprehensible parts of ourselves without shattering or becoming psychotic. While Perseus's magic mirror is not available to us on call, there is one that is.

Mirrors allow us safely to see terrible stuff by converting direct experience into indirect experience. What we see is not the actual thing but a reflection of it. It creates psychic space between us and the terrible thing. Indirect versus direct experience is seeing horror reflected by a movie rather than experiencing the actual horror. It's like the difference between being in a terrible accident or seeing it reflected on a movie screen. Indirect experience permits us to eat the wafer and drink the wine without experiencing the cannibal lying in the deeper layers of our unconscious.

There are numerous magic mirrors that can help us convert unbearable direct experience into more assimilable indirect experience. Dreams are an example of one of those mirrors. We wake up from a nightmare shaken but intact. In dreams we may experience tornadoes, hurricanes, earthquakes, jealous rage, snake bites, pursuit by crocodiles or panthers, heartbreak, profound disappointment, abandonment, and violence of all kinds. Yet we wake up essentially unscathed. Or in contrast we may experience profoundly ecstatic moments, stunning beauty and incredible feelings of love, and return to normal on waking. I remember one such dream. It was one of four "big" dreams I've had in my life. We Jungians call them "big" because they are so powerful that one can never forget them, no matter how much time elapses. And they feel as if they have touched and altered our lives indelibly in some way that we are unable to achieve by our own volition or will. Of all the dreams I have had, the following one was the most comforting and life altering:

In the dream, I was in a small, isolated farm house. The house looked as though it was made of rough, unpainted cedar. It had a small front porch with a few steps leading up to it. The house was not in good condition. It was very late at night or early morning. I heard a knock at the door. I opened the door and saw Jesus standing there on the front porch in an old, knee-length robe tied with a tattered rope around his waist. I asked him who he was. Jesus replied, "*Ich bin ein Berliner.*"

Most of us who are old enough remember these famous words spoken by President Kennedy during a visit to Berlin in 1963. Berlin at that time was like an island surrounded by hostile and threatening Russian forces. Kennedy represented a great power, a power much greater than Berliners felt themselves to be, that promised its support at a time of enormous stress and despair. Kennedy's words brought great comfort to Berliners. While his words did not remove the Berliners' fear, insecurity, and desperate feelings, it reduced them to a tolerable level by giving them hope and assuring them that they were not alone.

This dream had come at a time of considerable stress and despair in my life. Like the Berliners of those days, I felt threatened on all sides. I felt insecure and afraid. I was divided by conflicting thoughts and feelings. It felt as though my health, my finances, my relationships and my well-being were in perilous shape. The dream was an incredible comfort to me just as Kennedy's speech had been to the anxious Berliners. The dream, like Kennedy's speech, did not remove my daily fears and insecurities. But it ameliorated them. It felt as if I had been in a hurricane in which the winds died down from 120 miles per hour to 20, still uncomfortably windy but quite survivable. Another image that describes the change I felt from the dream is the image of an ocean, roiled and stormy on the surface and for several feet down, but calm in the lower reaches that are the bigger part.

This dream is a good example of converting what could be a shattering direct experience into an assimilable indirect experience. Dreaming of seeing God (Jesus) is most assuredly less awesome than actually seeing God, which, as I have discussed earlier, wise men have thought to be a shattering experience. While the dream left me with the inflated feeling of specialness, it is far less inflating than feeling that I am God. Being spoken to by God in a dream is less threatening to the moorings that ground us than the crazy thought that we actually are God. One brings us closer to God; the other identifies us with him.

This dream had an enduring influence on my life. I wish for more dreams of this power and beauty. Unfortunately, we have no control over dreams and can neither make them occur nor prevent them from occurring.

Symbols are also magic mirrors. They stand for the thing they reflect without being the thing itself. The wafer and the wine symbolize the blood and body of Christ but are not flesh or blood. Still, there is a hint that a cannibal lurks somewhere deep below, transformed by aeons of cultural and psychic development.

Writing in the third person can also provide a magic mirror. When writing in the third person, we can attribute both our light and our darkness to that third person, projecting onto them both the bright and the dark qualities that are in ourselves. It's one of the reasons that writing in the first person can be so difficult. Sometimes, if it were possible, I would write in the fifth person.

The magic mirror that is, perhaps, the most readily available to us is creative work, what we actually create, along with all the fantasies and images that precede the creation. Everything that we create is a magic mirror because it faithfully reflects ourselves, who we most deeply are, just as the creations of Monet, Picasso, Frank Lloyd Wright, Stravinsky, or Wagner reflected who they were. Their unique identity is expressed in their work, and we can recognize who produced it without seeing their signature. Even forgers' fraudulent products reflect their identity and can be recognized and detected by experts who study art. We leave an artistic fingerprint on all that we create that is as true to ourselves as our actual fingerprint.

In the past, I wrote most things in the third person. Writing as I am now in the first person doesn't feel safe. In previous writings, I not only felt more protected by writing in the third person, but I could also attribute some of the intimate poems and dreams included in this piece to anonymous patients.

Over time, the cumulative result of all our creative production is to reflect more and more of who we are. But no matter how much of our creative thought becomes manifest, much more remains unexpressed.

The magic mirror of creativity reflects us back to ourselves far more accurately than our parents could, even if they were exceptional. Parents could not reflect us accurately because they inevitably projected themselves onto us and saw themselves in us, their creation, just as we see ourselves in our creations.

As I reflect on this last point, I am becoming aware that while we actually are everything we ever thought, saw, heard, fantasized, or dreamed, we don't feel that big. We feel only as big as our continuing creative work, dreams, and other mirrors have made us consciously aware of. We know theoretically that we are much more than we are conscious of. The part we are unconscious of remains unconscious unless or until some awareness–altering insight comes to us.

In the end, all of our creations are self-portraits.[7] We see ourselves in them. It is this tendency of our creations to faithfully mirror ourselves that may

---

[7] These thoughts about the power of our creative work to reflect who we are are drawn heavily from the book, *Our Creative Fingerprint*, co-authored by my wife, Nancy Carter Pennington, and myself.

explain why, at some deep level, our creations repeat themselves in ever-recurring *leitmotifs* that run indelibly, like *roter faden*, through all our work. We repeat because our creative work can reflect only one thing, our selves. For each individual, this is a single, unique self. Ultimately, our art can only reflect our self and the particular issues, themes, and complexes that are important to it. The self is not interested in someone else's story and exerts enormous pressure to hold us to its own narrative. We can only manifest the particular "I am" that we are. Thus, if our work is to be true to ourselves, we must insistently repeat ourselves. Our creations are like acorns. They are a unique expression of the parental oak that produced them. The oak is to the acorn as we are to our art. Our art can no more be false to our self than an than an oak tree can be false to its acorn.

Artists are often aware of some underlying force that, like a powerful undertow, draws them tenaciously to a central story, despite conscious wishes they may have to do otherwise.[8] Some can give voice to the phenomenon. Speaking at a news conference after winning the 2014 Nobel Prize in Literature, Patrick Modiano, the French writer, described succinctly this tendency in himself: "I have always felt like I've been writing the same book for the past forty-five years." His words remind us of a conversation we had in Florence in 1998 at the Fourteenth

---

[8] Most of my writing has been about guilt and creativity. Thus, I similarly feel drawn to a central theme in all my work.

Congress for Analytical Psychology. We were speaking with a colleague when he asked us if we knew how many symphonies Vivaldi had written. Of course, we replied, "No." He smiled and said, "Four hundred, the same one four hundred times." In a well-known Swedish TV series, we see the middle-aged son of an artist asking his father why he always paints the same thing. The father says that each day he intends to paint something else, "Just splash the paint, see where it takes me. And then I start, and every time, I paint the same thing" (Cottan & Mankell, 2009).

The proclivity of artists to repeat themselves is also portrayed humorously in a story about Winslow Homer, a famous American seascape painter. A wealthy American reportedly asked Homer to paint his portrait. Homer refused, saying he only painted seascapes. The wealthy man persisted and finally offered Homer $5 million to paint his portrait. Homer agreed, but warned his patron not to be surprised if the painting looked like a seascape. Ultimately, as Jung once said, "We remain obstinately ourselves."[9]

I take some comfort from these thoughts when I realize my writing tends always to devolve into discussions of guilt or creativity. Of course, there is a relationship between those two subjects. When innovations in art and theory first appear, they often violate conventional norms, norms approved by the authorities. The Impressionist school of painters and

[9] This quote, too, is from my memory of what was said in a Jung Institute-Zürich lecture.

Darwin's theory of evolution are two examples of scientific and artistic developments shunned by religious figures and artistic critics of the day. From very early in life, we experience guilt when we do things that authorities, initially our parents, disapprove of.

Some might observe recurrent patterns in the creative production of an artist and be critical, as in the comment about Vivaldi. They may interpret it as creative laziness or some kind of loss of creative inspiration. They may see the tendency to repeat as pejorative; I see it as, perhaps, the supreme compliment. Because our creations reflect and mirror ourselves, creative work that permits us to see and express ourselves again and again from widely differing angles and perspectives is essential both to self-discovery and the deep and richly meaningful art that flows from it. This may be why Cezanne would paint the same landscape on consecutive days just minutes apart or why Frida Kahlo painted numerous self-portraits. While artists may not be consciously aware of the self-discovery purpose of their works, as psychologists we know this to be a powerful motivating urge.

The increase in self-discovery that the piece I am now writing not only makes me feel bigger and fuller, but also worth more. It's as if the dream, the fantasies, and the writing have filled an empty space in me that previously made me feel alone and worth only what an empty space is worth. Psychologically, feeling empty is a symptom of an early wound, of the so-called "narcissistic wound." One of the most important causes of the empty feeling is harshly critical parenting that severely limits how much of ourselves is allowed to be seen or expressed. A physical analogy to this psychic condition can help us understand the phenomenon. Imagine yourself owning a seven-room house. Mother and father come for a visit. They are very critical of all the furnishings in three of the rooms. In order to keep their approval and love, we empty these rooms of the furnishings and put them in the basement. Thus, part of our house is empty. We hide important parts of ourselves in order to preserve parental approval. The empty feeling of the house remains until we can bring the furniture back upstairs. Each piece of furniture we restore makes the house feel fuller again. We began life psychically whole. Everything was there *in potentia*. Very soon, however, as socialization began, we cleared out more and more rooms. Some rooms were never built at all. The degree to which rooms were emptied or not built depended upon the harshness of criticism by parents and other authorities.

I know it sounds a bit crazy, but I like this feeling of being fuller that writing this piece has provided, even if it is like a balloon filled by hot air. I like the feeling, although I suspect that one day some prick will come along, puncture the balloon, and cause it to collapse. Of course, death may serve as the deflating prick, unless some sharp critic has beaten the grim reaper to it.

The desire to escape my feeling of emptiness reminds me of another powerful dream I mentioned earlier. I was waist deep in a large bidet furiously washing away urine that had stained me. The washing away of the urine felt cleansing, a baptism of sorts. As I indicated earlier, the dream led me to write a story in which the Arch of Triumph was torn down and replaced with a giant gold bidet.

Like my other dreams, this one has both inner and outer meanings. The Arch is one of France's most visible and best known monuments, splendidly reflecting France's past glories and achievements. It was erected at the zenith of French world power. It doesn't reflect what France is today. Tearing the Arch down and replacing it with the lowly bidet expresses something that is valid both for societies as a whole and for individuals. It's about letting go of past achievements and living in the present, with who we are today as opposed to who we were yesterday. It's about accepting in our later years the more modest humans we've become and letting go of the pillars of the past. The tearing down of the Arch represents the challenge most of us face beginning at midlife until we die. The dream message was aimed much more at me than at France, true as it might be for them.

For many Frenchmen, replacing the arch with a bidet would be an irreverent, if not obscene, degrading, and contemptuous thought. Patriotic Frenchmen would hit the streets, if necessary, to halt such a project, which they'd resist with all their hearts and minds and souls. The "*gilets jaunes*" riots would seem mild by comparison. I might not feel safe in Paris if I were to publish such a story. Well, perhaps the Algerian/Muslim community might appreciate the deprecation of the French superiority that the arch proclaims. But they would definitely be in the minority.

The bidet dream may have an inner meaning that is important to me in another way. It isn't too difficult for me to suspect that the dream is an attempt by my psyche to forgive me my sins by washing them away. The bidet is used to wash the genitals and may be aimed specifically at washing away my sexual guilt which has weighed heavily on me most of my life. I think the seriousness of sexual trespasses was hugely amplified in my mind by the puritanical attitudes of my mother and grandmother. Their Victorian views didn't keep me from sex but did lay a heavy burden of guilt on me. In modern times sexual guilt is less conscious. But Queen Victoria still lingers in the unconscious, if not the conscious, minds. In the case of my generation, many of my friends and I were influenced and conditioned by openly puritanical attitudes and views. I felt ashamed of sex and masturbation. It didn't keep me from having sex or enjoying it at the moment, but waves of guilt would sweep in afterwards and affect the way I felt about myself and my worth. I can remember at some of the rare family gatherings, hearing whispered jokes about my grandmother having had four children without my grandfather seeing her undressed. In subsequent generations, especially after the so-called sexual revolution, conscious attitudes were much more accepting of sex, and the subject was more openly discussed. But Victoria was still there.

I remember working analytically with a young Italian male. He had many sexual hang-ups that made him unhappy. He said his mother was quite modern in her views but that when he sat next to her watching TV, she would without any word simply switch the channels when a sexual scene occurred. She thought she was protecting her young son. There are many nuanced ways, like switching channels, that sexual guilt enters our unconscious. When it does, we feel dirty after sex. We feel guilty as if we are bad persons. I suspect that this unconscious guilt accounts for some of the drive for great achievement and glory in our conscious lives. By becoming successful and admirable in our outer lives, we try to compensate for the guilty feeling of failure and worthlessness in our unconscious inner lives. I can remember clearly that after sexual escapades I often afterwards would enter into a phase of frenetic work and output. I think I was trying to do something good to make up for something bad.

I probably had a deep need for a psychological baptism that could help me feel forgiven, not only for my sexual trespasses, but for all the others mother frowned upon. Because love and blame cannot coexist, I cannot love myself until I can forgive myself. And until I can love myself, I cannot be fulfilled. All those rejected parts of myself that I was taught to hate will remain in my psychic basement, and the rooms they once filled will be empty. And I will feel empty to the degree that I cannot love myself.

In retrospect, it now seems possible that the iron grip of mother's definition of success as meaning wealth, as amplified by something in me, may have slowly begun to weaken at midlife as therapy, dream work, journaling, and other writing began the process of restoring to its original fullness the space that had been emptied by disapproval. And, perhaps, her definition of success that was symbolized by an impressive outer mansion is gradually being modified by a definition of success that gives at least some weight to the building of a richer inner structure. Many times in my life I have felt ashamed of my need to live my mother's values, that is, to be wealthy in order to become someone of worth, or appear to be wealthy in order to give others the impression of wealth or status. But I would also feel ashamed of being or appearing to be poor. That's why I often pretended to have more money than I actually did. It sometimes feels to me that the working of fate has carried me to a point in life where I am somewhat less, but certainly not completely so, driven either by a hope for fame and riches or a fear of poverty and insignificance. What I have been seeking, "that look" of approval that I once received from my mother, is, of course, something that transcends the opposites of riches and poverty or fame and insignificance. "That look" gives us a brief moment in which we experience and are momentarily in tune with our self.

Another way we can get tuned to our self and experience the feeling of "that look" is very similar to tuning a piano. To tune a piano, we find middle C, usually at 440 MHz. Then, we tune all the other notes in relation to it. Middle C is the point where the piano is perfectly tuned and in harmony with itself. It is to the piano what the self is to us.

In the first half of life, we tend to think we *are* middle C, that everything else in the world is in relation to us and depends upon us, when in truth we are actually a note way down the scale. That thought is, of course, unconscious, an unconscious wish that isn't true but causes us to behave as if it were. We can make a lot of music that way, and some of it may be pretty good music at that. It's just off, maybe by a hair, but still off.

It takes an illness or some sort of failure, like our music being rejected, severely criticized, or disparaged by someone else's music, to humble us enough for us to realize we're not middle C, that we're out of harmony not only with others, but also ourselves. We can probably never in this lifetime get as well-tuned as a piano, but we may get closer with advancing age, experience, and humility. Only when we realize how out of tune we are to ourselves do we have a chance to make adjustments, get more in tune with ourselves. In other words, we first have to realize that the tune we are singing is not our song. With this realization, a slow process of change may occur in which we gradually move closer to tuning to middle C.

Often in gangster movies we hear a mobster say he is going to tune someone up. I usually smiled at the phrase even though it was late in life before I knew what it meant. Inevitably the mobster was talking about tuning up someone who had betrayed or failed to do what the boss wanted. And the purpose of tuning someone up was to get them back in tune, back in proper relationship with the boss, making the boss, rather than themselves, middle C.

I remember attending a Maharishi seminar. He was the guru of transcendental meditation, or TM. This was soon after I had gotten sober, and I was looking for other ways of being. In practicing transcendental meditation, you are instructed to sit comfortably, with your eyes closed, and wait until the mantra begins. Then you repeat the mantra until you lose it and find yourself in this transcendent space that feels wonderful, a space beyond waking consciousness. Repeating the mantra eventually takes you to your self. Someone asked Maharishi what to do if the mantra doesn't begin on its own. Maharishi used the computer as an example. He said, "You have to press a button, and then it starts up and works for you as long as you follow its rules." He also talked about the best way to push the button and start the process. After you've closed your eyes and are ready for the mantra to come, Maharishi suggested you simply say something like, "Thy will be done." "Thy will be done" represents a change in attitude. It moves you out of the center, so you no longer feel that you are middle C. The ego shrinks, the mantra begins, and something bigger then takes over. The mantra is like a tuning fork that takes you to your middle C.

Later in life we often get out of tune. But once we've experienced the feeling and beauty of middle C, we never forget it, and, when we realize we are out of tune with it, we always want to get back to it. The feeling that goes with being tuned to middle C and the feeling that goes with seeing "that look" have a lot in common. They are both an experience of our self.

Writing this piece has, in many ways, been an effort to arrive at my own middle C, at my self. Suppose for a moment that my big dream about Eighteen East

74th Street had actually been realized and I had been able to live the life I fantasized. My hunch is that this piece would have never been written. Too much time and energy would have gone into all the details necessary to actualize that fantasized life. Everything I've written here would have remained unsaid. And I would be the poorer for it. The truth is that the actual life I live today in a modest home in Ardmore, Oklahoma, provides far better conditions for writing and other creative work than the splendid life in Manhattan would. Our only neighbors are a strip mall on one side, a couple of stores in front (including Maria's Garden, a world-class gift shop surprisingly found in the boondocks), a parking lot behind, and an empty house on the other side. We have almost no interaction with the neighbors. We have virtually no social life. We don't entertain. We are retired. Seldom does someone come to the door. From a privacy standpoint, it is almost like being deep in the woods. It's an almost perfect and propitious setting for me to think, feel, and write. From time to time, I've caught myself fantasizing about an actual hut in the woods where Nancy and I would be living, a place sparsely furnished with a bed, a couple of chairs, a small stove, and two writing tables. Sometimes Nancy and I write pieces together. We've found a way to keep our separate voices and also express them as one. We can sing duet or solo. This whole woodsy thing can feel quite beautiful in its simplicity. However, at eighty-eight, with all my medical issues and physical limitations, I need to be nearer doctors and an emergency room. Inside our present house, it still feels a bit like being in the woods while also being near a hospital. About the only thing that interferes with my creative work here is the tasks of daily living. I may sit down at my computer to write and the idea will pop into my mind that the dishwasher needs emptying or the trash needs to be taken out or I need to answer an e-mail from my daughter or a friend. Both the writing and the interference with it lie inside me. I don't believe that mansion and its glamorous lifestyle would have solved these problems or enriched my life the way this piece has. If the dream came true at all, it had to have come true somewhere inside me, since I didn't get the house. As I wrote earlier, achieving only an inner benefit would have been a great disappointment to mother. Well, to be truthful, it's a disappointment to me, but not crushingly so, as I also see its benefit in a sense of personal enrichment.

After the initial glamour and the thrill of "that look" from friends had worn off, I'm having a hard time imagining how the rich life in that mansion would have made life better. It wouldn't remove the aches and pains that go with my advanced age. I'd get just as angry at what I see on TV. I'd still have congestive heart failure, osteoporosis, atrial fibrillation, peripheral neuropathy, periodic skin cancers, an enlarged prostate and frequent urination, diminished hearing and eyesight, sleep apnea (along with my CPAP and its nuisance factor), daily pain from my broken back, daily pills galore, and a big home pharmacy to go with us when we travel. I'd still eat the same food, follow the same exercise program, and, of course, experience the same episodes of forgetting what I went into the other room for. And then, if we had the mansion and the life that went with it, there would be the additional burden of having to look after the real estate, the money, and all the stuff that we wanted and had acquired. It's true I could afford some help to care for all of it, but I'm sufficiently paranoid to have to check up on the helpers and their work. I might also worry about Nancy or me being abducted for ransom. Would we need bodyguards? Would that actually quiet the fears? Would my anxieties and insecurities go away? Would friends or family actually like me more? Probably not. I'm not sure a glamorous setting would do much to ameliorate any of these problems. Well, maybe a bit.

Because, deep down, who am I kidding? Here I am touting all the positives that flow from not having gotten the big house, the opulent life, and "that look" that I absurdly hope for. I'm making a virtue of creating a mirror in which to better see myself by writing this piece. I'm asserting that creative work will provide a mirror in which I can give myself "that look" and free myself of dependence on mother or others for supplying it for me. Closer to the truth, I suspect, is the likelihood that I have followed this writing path mainly because I didn't win the lottery and because of the kind of seizure that makes me write as described below. Fate intervened in a way that caused me to write this piece instead of leading the opulent life. Failure to win the lottery didn't free me of the need for "that look"; it just caused me to look elsewhere. If I had won the lottery, I am pretty sure I would not have had the Christ-like strength that I would have needed to resist the temptation to create the splendid material life offered by my dream, which gave me hope of getting "that look." If I had won the lottery, I feel pretty sure I would have pursued that life of splendor, rather than the writing life, to provide me the mirror I sought. The Devil would have been more persuasive to me than he was to Christ. But I didn't win the lottery, and something bigger than mother or me seems to have taken over and empowered me to write. The energy to write comes on me like a seizure. When it comes, I have to write. I can neither start it nor stop it by an act of will. While I want the writing to be good, the inner drive to do it doesn't seem to care so much about style or what others think of it. I care, but it wins.

I'm now thinking that there is nothing a human can do in this life to repeat "that look" that was once bestowed by mother. Because mother is the first image of God, "that look" can never be achieved again until, perhaps, our dying breath, when once again we may see the face of God. Between that first look and the last one, we try to do everything we can imagine that might bring "that look" again. As I wrote earlier in my poem, *Déjà Vu*, after I lost "that look," I looked ten thousand places and turned over ten thousand stones in order to find it again. We don't find it again, though, because it doesn't belong to us; it belongs to God. And he apparently withholds it till the end, which leads me to conclude that the initial giving of "that look," followed by the prolonged withholding of it, is the source of Divine Discontent. It's why nothing satisfies us between the initial look and the final one.

If we could be satisfied by something less, we would likely stop creating. Satisfaction is the enemy of creation. My suspicion is that the Creator wants us to create until we die. To accomplish his goal initially, through mother as surrogate God, he gives us a free sample of the dope ("that look") and then withholds it till the end. In that way, we never in our lifetime completely win the battle for deliverance from the Mother/God. Like the witch in fairy tales, she is never satisfied with the job we do. Neither is God. Well, God may allow us to experience satisfaction temporarily for brief spurts. That keeps us hoping for a permanent state of satisfaction, but, of course, that never comes while we are alive. Those brief spurts and the great pleasure that goes with them is probably what keeps us trying.

All of this makes me think back on the life of Ernest Hemingway. He strove mightily to reach the pinnacle of a writer's achievements. He won the Nobel Prize in Literature. Then, he killed himself. If one reaches the highest achievement one can possibly imagine in this lifetime and doesn't get "that look," I'm wondering if one doesn't just give up in despair and, then, as Hemingway did, do the only thing left to get "that look," or at least the thing that ends the search for it. Or perhaps what became unbearable to him was the opposite of "that look," the frowns of the literary critics and others who might not completely adore his writings and give him the unqualified approval for which he yearned. Perhaps, we're kept alive by thinking or, at least, hoping that there is still something we can do to get "that look." As psychologists, we know the dangerous moment is when there is no hope.

In *The Old Man and the Sea*, I suspect the old fisherman, humble as he appeared to be, had cathected that big fish earlier in life and spent his life trying to get "that look" by catching it and showing it off in his village. He did catch it, but before he could bring it back, the sharks ate it. Nothing was left but the skeletal bones. It's what happens to a lot of us at midlife. We've attained something we have long yearned for and sought. We've fought hard for something and gotten it. But once we have it, it turns out to be an empty shell, like the big fish. It doesn't give us the recognition and approval we want. It just feels empty, and all we thought it would mean to us is not there. If he had brought the big fish home, he would have felt he was a big man in the village. He would have felt he was really somebody. He would have felt recognized and respected and admired. If he had reeled in that big fish and brought it to the village, he may have felt that he'd found peace, that he'd finally come home, or so it might seem. He cathected a big fish. I cathected a big house. In the end, he felt totally exhausted by the effort, but he was alive. I'm feeling pretty exhausted, too. But I can't give up the ray of hope that, perhaps, Hemingway couldn't experience. At least, so far I have hope. If it weren't so tragic, it might be funny. Almost every day I check the numbers on the lottery tickets. At that moment, I'm not thinking about the almost impossible odds, the one in three hundred million, less probable than being struck by lightning. My eye catches a glimpse of a number on my ticket that corresponds to the power ball or the mega ball. It's like a tug on the fishing line. For a tiny moment you think you may have the big one on the line. It's usually a very small thing that sets off the obsession and the feeling that goes with it. The line tightens slightly, the reel clicks, and I have an ecstatic moment. I may have hooked the big fish, or in my case the big house. It's the feeling an alcoholic may get from seeing a beer commercial. You see or feel the thing, but it's not the thing. It's just a slight promise of the thing that sets you off. While the brief feeling you get is ecstatic, it is also fleeting. And it doesn't matter whether that feeling goes with something that is good or bad for you. After that brief moment of arousal, you likely end up with the feeling I do when I look at the rest of the numbers. *Rien du tout.* Big disappointment. I won two bucks. I don't get the house to show off. I'm left with the empty shell. Then, I feel how stupid I am to spend money on these tickets. Flushing the money down the toilet has about the same chance of winning something as spending it on the tickets. But not quite. Down the toilet is no hope. Buying the ticket is some hope, infinitesimal as it is. But a ray of hope is a ray of hope. An infinitesimal ray is better than nothing, I say to myself. And I keep buying the tickets. Thank God I can still afford them. I don't like to think of being too poor to buy a ticket. There was a time when that was true. In those days of real poverty, I, fortunately, didn't even know about things like the lottery.

The experience of Hemingway and other artists with tragic ends gives evidence that nothing is a panacea for all the wounds that life can bring us. Our efforts reach out in so many directions—creative work, living in grand houses, getting the Nobel Prize, catching the big fish, winning at cards. These all have a kind of symbolic equivalence in the momentary feeling they produce, but none fulfills the wishes we have to know ourselves. While I doubt now that creative work can in this life be a mirror that is magic enough to reflect us as totally and ecstatically as that initial look from mother, I know it can, more than any other mirror humanly available, help us see more of ourselves and make us much fuller, even if not completely fulfilled. Maybe all that is salvageable is an inner phenomenon of growth that can be recognized and appreciated only by me. Despite all that value, despite all the fulfillment that the inner work might bring, however, I'm still incapable of totally surrendering my hope to be recognized and appreciated on the outside. Perhaps part of the difficulty of totally surrendering the need for recognition from the outside is a lingering skepticism as to whether some of the things I learn about myself on the inside are worth it.

Despite conflicting doubts, and the exhaustion from trying that I sometimes feel, and despite my ambivalent wish that I could just let go of this deep, persistent need, I still harbor the notion that there is something more to be achieved through my writing. Even the wildly impossible probability of winning a Pulitzer for something I may yet someday write has grazed my mind. (See? She's still running the show, laughably so.) It's very hard to let go of at least trying to get some outer acclaim, despite my growing doubt that I can achieve enough to get "that look," especially since I believe that getting "that look," the real one, a second time, likely comes only at the end. But, perhaps unlike Hemingway, I still have some tiny hope supported by a fragile but enduring faith that struggles against the highly improbable. I still want the house. But the house is not really the thing that I want. It's "that look." But "that look" is not really the thing either. The real thing is the feeling that goes with "that look." That's what set off this whole process that has utterly exhausted me. I'm beleaguered by being pulled out to sea by the fantasies and the hoped-for re-encounter with that feeling. It's what happens to anybody who is addicted to anything. It's what happens when you fall in love. God's in charge. And you can't stop God. After many years of experience with my own addictions and the addictions that many of my patients struggled with, I have come to suspect our addictions are attempting to lead us to God. But we have to encounter many false gods before we get to the real one. It's kind of like people's experience with John the Baptist. They thought he was the one. He filled them with hope and high feeling. But he wasn't the one. He was the precursor of the one, the prophet who prepared the way for the one, who made his paths straight.

Basically, all this time and effort and suffering have left me half-empty, assuming the outside counts for something. I didn't land the big house or the fantastic things that go with it that, combined, would, at least as I imagine it, have gotten me that you know what. Sadly, it reminds me a bit of a snipe hunt in that it always ends with an empty gunny sack. My goal now is not to change, but to continue to become increasingly more conscious of who I have become.

In many ways, I'm ending life disappointed, because I didn't come close to what I earlier viewed as my promising future. A lot of friends, teachers, acquaintances, and, of course, family members thought I'd do something great, become rich, powerful, or famous, or perhaps all of these things. Certainly, they thought I'd do much better than my father. I know I hoped so. Still, those outside my family probably didn't really care or give the matter any thought when it didn't happen. I was the one who was deeply disappointed in myself. On the other hand, I don't think God was disappointed. I suspect I turned out pretty close to the way God wanted me to from the beginning.

The torrential flow of thoughts, feelings, memories, and fantasies that the dream of Eighteen East 74th Street triggered have slowed to a trickle. This movie seems near its end. No doubt others will come as new dreams stir the silt at the bottom of my pool. As I wrote this piece, the silt roiled by the Eighteen East 74th Street dream began to settle, and the pool cleared enough for it to reflect parts of my image that had not been so clear to me. It feels to me that this clarification has filled some empty space inside with some very old pieces of psychic furniture that had been stored earlier, out of sight and out of mind, within my psychic basement. While I feel somewhat larger now, I still do not feel fulfilled, and I probably never will. And it feels that the distance I've covered is less than the distance left to go. Time is running out. The creative process that this piece exemplifies will no doubt continue as new dreams come and attempts are made to write myself into further understanding. I have no idea what contents this process will help me restore or what new vistas it might supply. I'll write even if I may be reluctant to reveal the results to others.

In the end, I do need to acknowledge the truth that no one really knows who I am. I don't really know who I am. No one knows for sure who anyone is. As I wrote in the preface, who I am is basically who I imagine myself to be. I am a product of my own imagination and as such the result of some kind of creative process. I know, as Mailer pointed out, that the attempt to see and know who I am involves an inner dialogue between an observer and the observed. One self is absorbed in studying the other self. Despite all the work and learning, I'm still not sure who the observer is. Is the observer the author of all the thoughts and feelings and images it observes, or is the observer, like what he observes, the product of some third entity that creates both observer and observed? It truly is complicated, sometimes exasperatingly so. I certainly haven't figured it out, but something in me, the one who I imagine myself to be, makes me keep trying. For what it is worth, I'm pretty sure I know more about who I am than others do, but I think that is damning me with faint praise.

Given the inner boost I experienced from writing this much-less-complete version of myself, and still holding out a little hope, I have thought that one way I might gain some modicum of outer recognition would be to write and publish a more complete version of myself and my story. In the end, however, the thing that clinched it for me was that it would be a lot easier to confess openly to screwing a goat than to admit publicly all that the longer version of my story might contain. I'm becoming suspicious that only God could have created this beautiful, ugly mess that I am. I accord him all the blame and all the credit for his creation. In the end, I am beginning to think everyone and everything is a beautiful but ugly mess, each in its own particular way. That may be why creation as a whole seems to me to be a beautiful and ugly mess. But with all these pretty words, here's the rub: I don't have any problem accepting its beauty; it's the ugly part I still can't stomach. But, at eighty-eight, I'm still working on it.

I'm still working on the ugly stuff and the dark stuff because they contain precisely those qualities which first brought forth from mama "that look." We got "that look" not when we had achieved great things but when we were utterly helpless, weak, dependent, incontinent, dirty, irresponsible, stupid, whiny, loud, impolite, self-centered, selfish, ill-mannered, and incompetent. We got "that look" and the heavenly feeling that went with it before we had achieved anything, before the good grades, the promotions, and the awards. We were poor. We had no possessions. And we were toothless, bald-headed, and, objectively, not so handsome or beautiful. How could we be so wrong? Paradoxically, the stuff we later thought ugly was what earlier brought forth "that look." In hindsight, it's hard to believe that earlier we could actually have been *le seul*, the only one, when we looked and behaved in ways that later got us the opposite of "that look." It seems very possible that achievement is overrated in terms of getting me what I really most deeply want in life, to be loved exclusively and unconditionally.

Jesus said that we must become as a child again if we are to enter the kingdom of heaven. I suspect the way "that look" made us feel may be very close to the way we imagine we would feel if we ever do enter the kingdom of heaven. The two feelings seem linked in the paradoxical reality of our experience. And if we live long enough, it seems nature herself returns us to that primal state of physical and mental poverty which first produced "that look."

Being the owner of Eighteen East 74th and the glorious life that goes with it would, in this view, be the last thing likely to bring "that look" so that I could genuinely experience its gift of wholeness. If I owned Eighteen East 74th today and got "that look," I would be suspicious that it reflected a love of what I'd achieved and possessed, rather than love of me. I wouldn't feel loved and adored. I would feel it was my grand house that was being loved. I would doubt my lovability because it's not me being loved; it's my wealth and status. Soon after we got "that look" for the first time and socialization began, we were taught to get rid of all those childish qualities. In my case I was taught that I must achieve wealth and respectability if I were to be loved. As I advance into old age, increasingly manifest those childish qualities again, and am stripped of wealth, health, and competent behavior, I just might, if I got "that look" now, believe that it was truly for the love of me.

There is, also quite paradoxically, a model for doubting our lovability even when we have all the qualities we have been taught are admirable. It's Yahweh, the Old Testament God. He clearly doubted his lovability despite the fact he was all-powerful, all-knowing, and owned the world he had created. Despite all his power, knowledge, and creativity, he was jealous and apparently thought he was so inherently unlovable that he had to threaten people with severe punishment if they did not love and worship him. In Exodus 20:1–5, the Bible states: "And God spoke all these words, saying, 'I am the Lord your God... You shall have no other gods before me ... for I the Lord your God am a jealous God, visiting the iniquity of the fathers upon the children to the third and the fourth generation of those who hate me'" (Revised Standard Version). But who is there for God to be jealous of? He wouldn't have needed to say this unless he believed there actually might be someone or something else that had desirable qualities that many might believe exceeded his own. Presumably, in the period of Exodus, that might have been ancient deities like Indra, Zeus, Marduk, Ra, or other gods. But this suggests that even Yahweh had inner doubts and was so insecure about his own lovability that he had to issue threats to get love. I wonder if Yahweh had a mother like mine, one he only half believed when she assured him that he could get "that look" again if he would perform and achieve at the highest level. Maybe that half belief was caused by the look of love early in his life that he felt and remembered as sweeter than anything he had yet experienced from all the power and wealth he had accumulated, from the perfection he had achieved. Maybe his achievements were an insurance policy to reassure him in case she was right. Perhaps Christ's statement that one must "turn and become like children" to enter the kingdom of heaven (Matthew 18:3, Revised Standard Version) refers to the need to return to the childish state that earned each of us "that look" from our own mothers.

As I wrote earlier, the feeling that comes from that look is so ecstatic, so powerfully indelible that we wish to have it only for ourselves, to be *le seul*, just as Yahweh did. It's a profound wish, embedded in an infant's unconscious, to maintain that gleam—and particularly the ecstatic feeling that went with it—that we saw for the first time in our mother's eyes as she looked at us adoringly, like the Magi or the Virgin Mary, with an unconditional love that suggests she's looking at something divine. She makes us feel that we are God. In our unconscious, we become like the Old Testament God: we become a jealous God. And, if we have our way, we will have no other gods before us. Of course, all these thoughts would seem crazy if they were conscious.

This unconscious wish is possibly behind much of the competition we see in life to be the best, to be number one. We hope to be number one because we believe it will earn us that feeling that we first experienced without having to earn it. The world creates gods to satisfy this deep need. We see it on ESPN. Program after program is devoted to discussing who is the best quarterback, the best defensive back, the best basketball player, the best baseball or tennis player, and on and on. CNBC and Forbes talk about who is the richest. We try to create royalty in all areas of our life.

What we don't see is the virtual impossibility of being acclaimed universally as number one. Many think Tom Brady was the greatest quarterback. Others think it's someone else. In basketball, is it Michael Jordan or LeBron or Kobe or someone else? Due to hidden assets or questions of valuation, it's almost impossible to determine who the richest person in the world might be. Deciding who is the greatest novelist or painter is even more subjective, making consensus nearly impossible.

All these competitors, whether in sports, wealth, the arts, or some other venue, have the same problem, exactly the one I imagine Yahweh had. Despite all their achievements and glory, they must have lingering doubts about their being number one. They have their doubts because there are others who are thought to be the one, just as Yahweh must have jealously noticed when he saw Aaron's golden calf. In life there will likely always be competing gods, heavens, and Promised Lands.

The futility of ever satisfying the wish to be number one is caused by the fact that it is others, not one's self, who decide. And others have disparate views. Being thought of as the one by a lot but not all of the people isn't even close to the ecstatic feeling of being number one that came from that exclusive unconditional look from mama.

In the end, one is helpless when it comes to being number one. But paradoxically, as I noted above, it is this very helplessness that originally got that look that made us feel we were number one. So, the lesson may be that that the helpless state, not our outer achievements, may be the very thing, that, if acknowledged, makes us feel we are number one. This may have been the condition of the Israelites when they were eventually allowed to enter the Promised Land. They were helpless by their own powers alone to sustain themselves in the wilderness. They had no food or water. They were dirty and irresponsible. They were whiny and ungrateful. They were like children. Moses had been the adult, yet he didn't make it to the Promised Land. In the end, he didn't get "that look." The whiny destitute children of Israel being allowed to enter the Promised Land may be a good example of high achievement being overrated. Helpless and underachieving as they were, when they entered the Promised Land they felt loved and accepted by God, just as a child does by mama's look.

The question of what gets us what we most want in life is related to the long-standing debate in Christianity as to whether it is faith or works that leads to salvation, to being loved and accepted by God. Mother is our first god, all powerful. Pre-socialization, her message is that helpless dependence and childlike faith in her are the qualities that gain her love and acceptance. Post-socialization, her message is that we have to work for these things, to achieve in ways acceptable to her. She also demands our love and devotion. We get a mixed message from her, just as we get a mixed message from Christianity. And the message we tend to believe for much of our life is the post-socialization message, the one that calls for achievement and conformity to her rules and values. We are torn between her words and her actions, what she says and what we have seen. This leads to a lifelong dichotomy, the tension we feel between our desire to believe what people say versus our skeptical concern that we'd better attend to what they do. Rhetoric can take our eye off the ball.

These thoughts are what lead me to my late-life longing to remember, not my achievements, but the raw, unpolished self who first received "that look" of adoration, which for the first and only time I experienced as love. Mother gave me "that look" without telling me I had to do anything to get it.

This does not mean that no one has ever loved me. Only they *know* whether or not they do, but my mind tells me I'm loved. It's just that I'm not likely to *feel* the genuineness of "that look" or other assurances of love until I receive it when I am in an advanced state of decrepitude, quite similar to the helplessness of childhood.

On the other hand, if by some great stroke of luck I actually got to live at Eighteen East 74th along with the splendid life that goes with it, I might be wise to be open to the possibility that life there might not be about love or being *le seul* at all, but about so much fun that I would get the glorious feeling that goes with "that look" without having to get the look at all. Walking in the door of Eighteen East 74th might feel like walking into the Promised Land. It could be a moment when the reel clicks. The heart beats faster. Feelings soar. Oh my! What a wonderful gift would that be for a very mischievous, grateful, and rapidly aging old man like me!

References

Azémar, F. & Krivine, F. (Writers), & Triboit, P. (Director). (November 28, 2010). *Notre père* (Season 3, Episode 2) [TV series episode]. In L. Cavalier (Executive Producer), *Un village Français.* MHz Networks.

Churchill, W. (1951). *The Second World War, Volume V: Closing the Ring.* Boston: Houghton Mifflin Company.

Cottan, R. & Mankell, H. (Writers), & Martin, P. (Director). (May 10, 2009). Sidetracked (Season 1, Episode 1) [TV series episode]. In K. Branagh, R. Eaton, and A. Fernandez (Executive Producers), *Wallander.* BBC Video.

Faulkner, W. (2019). *The Sound and the Fury.* New York: Modern Library.

Ibsen, H. (1976). *The Wild Duck and Other Plays.* New York: Modern Library.

Jung, C.G. (1989). *Aspects of the Masculine.* NJ: Princeton University Press.

Mailer, N. (1976). *Genius and Lust: A Journey through the Major Writings of Henry Miller.* New York: Grove Press.

Shakespeare, W. (2020, March 10). *The Tragedy of Macbeth.* The complete works of William Shakespeare. http://shakespeare.mit.edu/macbeth/full.html.